Praise for *Are You Psychic or Making It Up?*

"I truly enjoyed reading this book. I personally have spent years distrusting my own intuitive gifts and have found that when I merged the mystical part of myself with my more skeptical, scientific side, not only did my work as a doctor, teacher and author improve, but so did my personal life. Carole Lynne shows you how to merge the worlds in a beautiful and light way, offering you tools that will help you trust your experiences, dig deeper within yourself, and find the real truth hidden within your mystical gift."

—Eva Selhub, MD, author of *The Love Response* and *Your Brain on Nature*

"Carole Lynne's new book candidly explores many challenges for those with psychic abilities living in our society. Her advice related to finding a 'spirit friendly' therapist is spot on. As a clinical social worker with a private psychotherapy practice I agree with her concern that authentic psychics could easily be wrongfully diagnosed with mental illness by a therapist who is unaware of the spirit world and abilities of psychics. She goes on to give practical tips for finding the right kind of therapist to support and guide psychics who are also often more sensitive than others to the world around them. This book is packed full of insightful information that is discussed among psychics, and we are fortunate that Carole has taken the time to write this guide for psychics and their friends and family members."

—Cindy Williamson, licensed independent
clinical social worker

D1052572

"Add Carole Lynne's perspective on the unseen world to your world. In this book Carole Lynne illuminates a deeper understanding of what it means to be a sensitive in this world and the challenges and responsibilities of having psychic and mediumistic gifts.

"The experiences and wisdom she shares can provide readers with invaluable and trustworthy insights into their own spiritual happenings because her integrity as a Medium and dedication to a life of teaching shine through. I believe many will find comfort and guidance within these pages because we should all, sensitive or not, desire to live a more balanced life and to be more authentic in our actions.

"As a Reiki Master Teacher, Medium, and student of Carole Lynne, I know I will refer to her book in teaching my students how to develop themselves spiritually, personally, and as healers. I strongly recommend this book to those who are exploring their spiritual gifts, those who offer healing and messages to others already, and to their loved ones."

—Amanda de Rezendes

"In my 30 plus years of as a physician and surgeon, I have experienced many unexplained phenomena which have filled me with awe and wonderment. Some of these experiences I have considered coincidental or happenstance, but many more I have felt a part of directly whether they be influenced by what I was feeling or thinking or I had a significant effect on the predictions or outcomes. I truly feel I have witnessed miracles. My wife and I have always felt we have had guardian angels, perhaps even a troop of them, who have unfortunately had to work overtime to help us out of many situations.

"When we first read about Carole Lynne, then met her for mediumistic sessions, we began to understand our personal energies and gifts that helped make more sense of what transpired. We appreciated Carole's ability to help us understand that our religious beliefs were an integral part of these intangible 'feelings.'

"Her latest book will help many gain a better understanding and awareness of these qualities we all possess whether you call them 'intuition,' 'hunches,' 'coincidences' or 'psychic abilities.' For some readers, it may open up a whole new dimension of understanding and possibilities. Carole has my respect, admiration and support of this valuable work."

—Wendell P. Wong, MD

ARE YOU
PSYCHIC
OR MAKING IT UP ?

ARE YOU
PSYCHIC
OR MAKING IT UP ?

Understand and Manage Your
Psychic Self and Help Your Loved
Ones Who Think You May
Be Losing It

CAROLE LYNNE

WEISERBOOKS
San Francisco, CA / Newburyport, MA

First published in 2014 by Weiser Books
Red Wheel/Weiser, LLC
With offices at:
665 Third Street, Suite 400
San Francisco, CA 94107
www.redwheelweiser.com

Library of Congress Cataloging-in-Publication Data
Lynne, Carole.
Are you psychic or making it up? / Carole Lynne.
    pages cm
  ISBN 978-1-57863-562-7
1. Parapsychology. I. Title.
  BF1031.L79 2014
  133.8--dc23

                                        2014023339

Interior by Frame25 Productions
Typeset in Adobe Garamond Pro

Printed in the United States of America.
EBM
10 9 8 7 6 5 4 3 2 1

I dedicate this book to my core students:

Ron, Melissa, Barbara, Sirry, Amanda, Joe, James, and Stephanie.

May they continue to help others.

Acknowledgments

I express my appreciation and deep gratitude to my publisher Jan Johnson, who has stood by me through the writing of five books. She has received my calls and texts when I needed guidance in the development of each manuscript. Every writer appreciates how valuable it is to have guidance.

As I finish each book, I laugh and I cry. As authors, many of us share deeply, and when a book is done, it is as if a baby has been born. So again I say thank you, Jan, for going on this journey of the soul with me. You have been my publisher/midwife as each book has been born!

Contents

One: Understand Your Psychic Self   1

Read descriptions of the psychic and mediumistic experiences many of you have had: visions, dreams, out-of-body experiences, premonitions, mind-reading, and more. Gain perspective on how to deal with your spiritual gifts.

Two: Take Special Care of Your Psychic Self   35

Those of us who are psychic and mediumistic are more sensitive than the general public. As we pick up on the thoughts and feeling of others and receive messages from spirit, we can experience a psychic "overload." We need to take special care of ourselves and learn how to turn down the psychic stimulation.

Three: Managing Your Relationships with Others   57

Learn to be comfortable being your psychic self in a skeptical world. Manage your relationships to gain support of others, even if many do not believe you. Avoid seeking approval from everyone. Keep a low psychic profile at work unless you are working in a "spirit-friendly" environment.

Four: Finding the Helpers You Need

Opening up to psychic and mediumistic experience is a challenge. Even strong and emotionally stable people need help and guidance on this path. Learn how to find a good teacher, friends like you, and a "spirit-friendly" therapist.

Five: Carole Lynne's Personal Spiritual Toolkit

The cornerstones of Carole Lynne's spiritual life are Spiritualism's Principle of Personal Responsibility and the teachings of Sri Aurobindo and the Mother, founders of the Sri Aurobindo Society in Pondicherry, India. Carole Lynne's work as a spiritual channel, starting in 1987 and continuing today, connects her with what she names "The Energy" and "Guidance."

Organization Resources 135

About the Author 139

How Carole Lynne's Books Can Help You 141

Before You Read This Book, a Disclaimer

This book is not intended to take the place of advice from spiritual directors, doctors, psychologists, or counselors. The author is one woman—a psychic medium and spiritual teacher—sharing her experience. Carole Lynne reminds her students and all who read this book that spiritual experience does not take the place of medical help. If you have physical, emotional, or mental problems that require the help of medical professionals, get the assistance you need. If you ever have thoughts that tell you to do anything negative or if you feel any negative energy within the messages you are getting, you may be having an emotional experience or hallucination that needs immediate professional attention. Authentic spiritual experience is positive and uplifting.

Foreword

Carole Lynne has written a truly meaningful and poignant book for the multitude of psychically sensitive individuals throughout the world. Few books have ever been written by such a prominent and internationally known psychic medium who, rather than focusing on her own skill and success, shows a genuine care and concern for the students on a similar path of psychic development and enlightenment. She not only helps students understand that they are likely to be more sensitive to life than many others but also helps them to have compassion for their loved ones who may not understand their psychic gifts. She teaches all of us who are psychic and mediumistic how to accept our own gifts, and then how to diplomatically gain the support of our loved ones who may be less like us.

Carole Lynne's work in the United States and Europe has grounded her with the realization that navigating between the psychic world and everyday life can often be challenging for students new to the energy of Spirit. With this in mind, she offers concrete guidelines to ensure success along the path of psychic discovery. These activities are coupled with

Ms. Lynne's insistence on the importance of working with a teacher throughout the developmental process.

Carole Lynne gently leads the reader through chapters that resonate with those who are experiencing an awakening of psychic phenomenon within their lives. Her words lift the senses beyond the logic and reason that can render the student unable to reach the altered conscious state of psychic experience. She shows us that there is no room for the ego during the engagement of Spirit by the psychic medium.

Carole Lynne is not oblivious to skeptics who do not adhere to the reality of psychic phenomena. Rather than citing the voluminous research conducted by doctors and psychologists or the supporting normative data from law enforcement and government security programs, she instead expresses a heartfelt concern for those psychic practitioners who continually suffer attacks from the unaccepting public. The ability to access altered states of consciousness is not regarded as a theory to Carole Lynne but as fact. She encourages those of us with spiritual gifts to be grateful for those gifts and to use them wisely.

The inherent friction between the interface of psychic consciousness and science echoes many of the paradoxes inherent in Quantum Theory, i.e., "every particle of matter is attracted by every other particle of matter"; "during quantum experiments involving the measurement of electron matter, the act of observing the experiment alters it by simply adding the observer." While science seems eager to accept the ambiguities of quantum physics when it attempts to define matter and energy, it often frowns upon the work of the psychic mediums that are able to access energy by methods not yet investigated or proven by science.

I met Carole Lynne five years ago when my mediumship began to unfold. As a psychologist and medical educator working in an environment of cause and effect science, I was critical and unaccepting of the gift that I had been experiencing since childhood. Despite the evidence and accurate feedback I received, I continued to doubt. The lessons and guidelines reviewed in this book showed that my initial reaction was common to most mediums. Carole Lynne's experience and suggestions outlined in her book helped focus and guide me to my path as an evidential psychic medium. Nothing that I had learned during my doctoral education, career as an international educator, behavioral scientists or co-founder of a health care organization prepared me for the responsibility of serving others with the gift of mediumship. For this I am eternally grateful to Carole Lynne and extremely excited that others around the world will have the opportunity to be touched by her words.

Carole Lynne, who is an ordained minister, commissioned healer and certified medium in the religion of Spiritualism, has volunteered many hours to serve in churches in the United States and Europe. Above all, however, Carole Lynne is devoted to her family and community. While gifted with paranormal skills, she remains a normal, energetic and kind woman to all who are drawn to her as students. She travels extensively to teach and to participate in her family's charitable foundation that provides food for infants in India.

Carole Lynne is a compassionate and ethical woman who stresses to her students that being a medium is a sacred gift. It is not to be exploited as a sensational activity designed to excite the curious. The gift of mediumship is a stepping-stone on the medium's spiritual path, not the end of the journey. She reminds us that we are a spirit living in a physical body. As Carole Lynne writes in her closing poem, "find the seed of divinity in your soul."

This book will point the reader in the correct direction.

Dr. James Deary III, MA, ED.D.
Psychologist-Educator-Medium
North Palm Beach

Introduction

Am I Psychic or Making It Up?
Survival in a Skeptical World

We live in a skeptical world where those who do not have the psychic experiences that we have often think we are making up these experiences. In fact, we ourselves question whether we are making them up and starting to "lose it."

The truth is, there really *are* such things as psychic and mediumistic experiences. Our psychic gifts allow us to know things about others, and our mediumistic gifts allow us to communicate with the spirits of those who have passed on. My years of experience as a psychic medium and teacher have proven time and time again that I am *not* making it up. Having said that, it took me many years to be able to make this statement!

We need to not only understand the spiritual gifts we have been given, but also learn how to get along with others in our skeptical world. Let's face it—some of our best friends and lovers are non-psychics, and if we cannot get all of them to believe us, we want them to be supportive.

The good news is that *you can* understand yourself and *you can* communicate with many of your loved ones in a way that will encourage them to be supportive. As the saying goes, "you can't win 'em all." But I believe you can win most of them if you take the right approach.

I've spent decades adjusting to my psychic and mediumistic gifts—first as a student and then as a professional. I want to share with you the tools I have developed that enable me to live a balanced life *as* a psychic medium. I want to teach you how to educate your loved ones so that they understand you. While they may not accept your beliefs, you can encourage them to be understanding and supportive. *This is not an easy task, but it can be done.* I am doing it and you can too.

Balance must become our mantra. Say that word over and over. We who are spiritually gifted need to work at balance in our lives. We need to manage the special gifts, needs, and responsibilities that come as part of the package. After all, we *do* live in two worlds: we are aware of physical life on the earth plane *and* the eternal life of the spirit. *We have twice as much territory to manage.*

Many of you have been writing to me for years to let me know how **confused** you feel about the psychic experiences you have, how **alone and misunderstood** you feel when people in your life do not understand you, and how **traumatized** you are when it occurs to you that the special gift you have been given comes with huge responsibility. I know how you feel because I have been there. I have struggled up this mountain of confusion and gleefully reached the top. While I do not have all the answers, I have many of them. I have transformed from a young woman who ran away from her psychic and mediumistic gifts into an older woman who has accepted her spiritual gifts and is grateful for her ability to help others.

Now I have reached the part of my spiritual journey where I invite you to join me at the top of the mountain, where you can feel safe and happy to be psychic!

First, learn to understand yourself and the psychic and/or mediumistic experiences you have. *Second,* learn how to take special care of the sensitive person you are—body, mind, and spirit. *Third,* learn how to talk to your loved ones and friends about your spiritual experiences diplomatically, rather than running into the living room screaming at the top of your lungs that you see a spirit in the basement. *Fourth,* learn to get the help you need from teachers both inside and outside of the Spiritualist community. Also learn how to evaluate whether you need additional emotional help from what I like to call a "spirit-friendly" therapist.

As you learn, you will be better able to make a decision about *how you do or do not* wish to share your spiritual gifts. Some may want to use their spiritual experiences only to enhance their personal lives. Others may want to help others in addition to helping themselves. The goal of this book is to help you understand your gifts, find the education you need, and learn to talk to your loved ones. Believe me: you CAN learn to survive in a skeptical world.

You're Part of Our Psychic Community. You're Not Alone!

You may be different, but you are definitely not alone. There are many others who have both psychic and mediumistic experiences in what I call "our psychic community." This is not a formal community where we wear nametags and badges. None of us would want to be part of that kind of community, right? I am describing a group of us who have similar spiritual experiences and challenges to cope with. We can help each other! Welcome to our club!

Every Community Has Its Language

As we work together I will be using terminology that might be unclear or unfamiliar to you. I want all of us to be on the same page, so to speak.

Understand from the get-go that the word "psychic" is used in many different ways. A woman doing tarot card readings may be described as a "psychic." Some use the word to describe the work of a medium—a person who communicates with the spirits of loved ones who have passed on. The "psychic experience" can mean anything from a spiritual dream to a premonition. Unfortunately, there is quite a bit of variation in the use of the word within the psychic community.

In this book I will use the word "psychic" as a general term that covers both psychic experience, mediumistic experience, dreams, and a range of other spiritual experiences. Sometimes I will distinguish between what is psychic and what is mediumistic. A psychic experience occurs when you have visions of people who are *living,* or receive information (of which you have no previous knowledge) for yourself or others through your psychic sense. When your experiences relate to information about or visions of *those who have passed on,* you are having what many in our profession call a "mediumistic experience." You will understand how I am using these two terms by the context in which I use them. For instance, when I am speaking about the spirit of a living person communicating with the spirit of another living person, this is a psychic experience. When I am speaking about the spirit of a living person communicating with the spirit of someone who has passed on, this is a mediumistic experience.

While it is important that you eventually understand the difference between a psychic and a mediumistic experience, you may not understand what you are experiencing when you are first opening up to the world of spirit. It will be difficult for you to try to attach the correct labels to your experiences too early in the process. Don't worry too much about labeling these experiences. For one thing, you will ultimately find that people around the world do not agree on the labels anyway. It is more important that you understand the *value* of each experience than it is to attach a label to it.

When I refer to what many name "God," I will use words such as Divine, Divine Consciousness, Spirit, Great Spirit, Guidance, and Source. For me, these words describe the same spiritual Source in the universe. We each come from different backgrounds and may use different terms to refer to the God of our understanding. Please use the name for God that speaks to *your* soul.

May I be your mentor?

Allow me to guide you as you learn to understand and manage your spiritual gifts while living in a skeptical world. Together we will make great progress! I invite you to take this journey of understanding spiritual experience with me. Let's begin.

ONE

Understand Your Psychic Self

OF COURSE YOU DO NOT understand what is happening when spirits that look like living people start appearing in your mind or in front of your face. Of course you are freaked out when you receive a message in your mind that tells you to slow down at the next intersection, and then you see a truck run the red light. You know if that message had not come to you, the truck would have hit your car.

Most of us who are psychic are understandably freaked out when the spirit world starts letting us know it is with us. The spirits are calling out to us, and if we are able to understand what is happening, perhaps we can accept our spiritual gifts and the "calling" we are experiencing. This is not a time to start thinking about so-called "spooky spirits," as we have gathered many of those scary images from TV and movies. If we can walk the spiritual path and not get caught up in the sensationalism that the word "spirits" brings to mind, this time many of us call "spirit knocking on your door" can be a period of spiritual transformation. Take a deep breath, know you are safe, and start learning about the experiences you are having.

Understanding Our Experiences

It is likely that you have had *some* of the experiences listed below, but not all.

- Visions of people who have passed on

- Vivid dreams of people who have passed on

- Out-of-body experiences where you feel your spirit is in another place or dimension

- Ability to read the minds of people around you

- Extremely empathic feelings for another person's physical or emotional pain

- Visions of the future that actually come true

- Feelings of dread when meeting certain people

- Warning messages in your mind or strong feelings that have saved your life or the life of a loved one

- Seeing a word in your mind that seems to appear everywhere you go

- Remarkable coincidences involving hearing songs in your mind or on the radio, TV, or Internet

- Objects moving inexplicably

- Objects appearing that were not there before

- Bells ringing for no reason, electric appliances that are not hooked up turning on, telephones and doorbells ringing with no explanation as to why or how

- Feeling that spirits are around you because the air feels "dense"

- Feeling as if a spiritual presence has touched you

- Songs or poems being composed by you in total, as if these pieces were simply "in the air" and all you did was reach up and grab them

- Feeling upset or elated after visits to spirit occupied locations (sometimes called "haunted" or "healing")

I could fill pages with these experiences. We will explore some of them now.

Three Important Guidelines

You may feel quite confused and overwhelmed when you have your first psychic experiences. Knowledge is power. As you understand your experiences, you will be empowered to cope with the unusual things that are happening to you and around you. The following guidelines will help you evaluate each experience.

Guideline One: First Look for a Logical Explanation

Every time you have a psychic experience, first look for a *logical* explanation of the experience. For example, that light going off and on in the hallway without anyone touching the switch may be caused by a short in the wire and not by a spirit. Observe the pattern created as this light goes on and off. Does the light seem to blink when you talk about a certain subject? If you say out loud "If you are a spirit, please prove it to me by blinking on the count of three: one, two, three, blink," does the light blink? Be a good spiritual detective, and do not automatically scream, "There is a spirit here!" each time a light does something unusual. I would not assume that I was communicating with a spirit if the light did not respond to me in a way that made me feel there was an intelligence of some kind communicating with me.

The bell you hear ringing inside your living room, where there is no physical bell present, may in reality be a church bell in the distance and not an angelic sound. I hate to say it: when you can't find your car keys and you are sure that a spirit moved them from the coffee table (where you left them) to the kitchen counter (where you finally found them), it may be that you simply forgot where you left your keys. The world of spirit has nothing to do with it.

Don't be discouraged by my skepticism. We will be exploring what happens when an authentic psychic or mediumistic experience occurs. I am sure you agree that you do not want to say you have received a communication from the world of spirit before you explore the many possibilities of how an experience may have been created.

Too Many Unexplained Experiences?

Many of us have come to the conclusion that indeed, some experiences *cannot* be explained logically. When the source of the sound of that bell cannot be explained logically, *then* you may want to consider whether you are hearing an angelic sound.

Once, when I was first opening up to the world of spirit, I heard incredible music in the living room. I assumed a radio was on. The only problem was, I could not *find* a radio! I asked my husband, who was sitting next to me, "Honey, is the radio on? Do you hear the beautiful music?" He looked at me strangely and said he did not hear a thing. By now, many years and psychic experiences later, when I say I am hearing beautiful music and he does not hear anything, he simply asks, "What are they playing today?"

Guideline Two: Allow Yourself a "Yup Moment"

When a possible psychic experience cannot be explained logically and you have a strong sense that spirit is communicating with you, you can legitimately allow yourself to have a "Yup moment," as in "Yup, this is *not* a coincidence." Psychically, you may be tapping into another level of reality or entering a different dimension than you ordinarily live in during a "normal" day. I don't want to say that we psychics have abnormal days, but I will say we have extra-sensitive days, when very unusual things happen. Yup, we sure do!

Guideline Three: Do an Ego Check-In

As you have psychic experiences, check in with your ego every now and then to make sure it is not making you feel like a superstar. It is all too common for those of us who are discovering our psychic natures to have *ego expansion attacks.* We start thinking we are special, unique, and better than other people. We may even start to see the stars of Hollywood in our minds and dollar signs in our dreams. "There I am on TV, the most famous psychic in the world." Or "There I am being flown to Europe to meet with royalty because they want a reading with me."

We are *not* better than other people because we are psychic. Repeat this to your ego over and over. People have different talents. Some are incredible football players; others are talented musicians; some are brilliant students. If you are psychic and/or mediumistic, this only means that you have a *particular* talent. Unfortunately, the general public is fascinated by anyone who is psychic, so it becomes all too easy for us to get big heads. As my mother always used to say, "Watch it, kid." Allow me to be your psychic mama and tell you to watch out for your ego. Ego check done, psychic mama lecture over.

Dreams, Out-of-Body Experiences, Premonitions, and Visions of Those Who Have Passed On

Dreams

My dreams fall into four categories: junk dreams, vivid dreams, lucid dreams, and nightmares. Compare your dreams to mine. Do you have similar kinds of dreams?

Junk Dreams

I invented the term "junk dreams" for my regular, every night kind of dreams. *All* the junk of the day shows up in these dreams. When I wake, I feel as if my brain has been trying to process things that have happened to me or that I have been thinking about. The colors in these dreams are not vivid and I do not hear music. Often the storylines are very confusing. When I am anxious, there are several recurrent themes: losing my handbag, getting lost, and realizing I never graduated from high school. I am not one to try to understand junk dreams. I'm not drawn to reading books that interpret the meaning of dreams. However, if you are interested in analyzing your everyday junk dreams, you will find many books and professionals specializing in dream analysis.

Vivid Dreams

These dreams are *amazingly* brilliant: they are always in color and make me feel as if I am traveling into spiritual realms that are very different from the environment I am used to living in. Often I feel like I am flying above landscapes of vivid shades of green and lakes and skies painted an iridescent blue. Sometimes I see people I have known who have passed on into eternal life. Other times I see people or figures I have never known who have spiritual messages for me. I wake up knowing I have been in a beautiful place. Sometimes I feel warm all over, as if I have been hugged by the universe. What a wonderful feeling!

I receive a vivid dream as a spiritual gift. I wish I could have them regularly, but they do not come to me that often. Naturally, I pay more attention to vivid dreams than junk dreams. The messages I receive are often important: they cause me to transform and change my life. If you are interested in learning about my important spiritual dreams, read my book *Cosmic Connection: Messages for a Better World.*

If you have a vivid dream, when you wake up, *immediately* write down any messages that came to you. If you saw beautiful sights, make drawings. I am so glad that I documented my important spiritual dreams. Every time I look at the notes and pictures of my vivid dreams, I am able to recall the dream and how I felt when I woke up.

Lucid Dreams

These dreams are also vivid, but there is an important difference. I am dreaming, yet I am *awake* within the dream and can say to myself "Oh, I am dreaming." I can see my physical body lying on the bed while I experience my spiritual body flying over a vivid scene within my dream. I am having what many call a "lucid dream."

I have dream-traveled as near as the rooftop next door and as far as distant planets or spiritual realms that are not material in substance. People who have passed on and spiritual guides come into these dreams. They are working to help me with my spiritual development. I often hear beautiful music that is unlike any earthly music I have ever known. I wake from these dreams knowing that my spiritual body has traveled into realms apart from the earth plane. Sometimes, at the points when these dreams begin and end, I feel a wind pass over me as my spiritual body leaves my physical body. I feel the wind again when my spiritual body re-enters my physical body. I do not have these special dreams very often, but when I do, they are transcendent experiences.

If you are interested in learning more about lucid dreams, read books on both lucid dreams and out-of-body experiences. My favorite author on this subject is Rick Stack. I first read his books and attended one of his workshops in the 1980s. Do an Internet search for Rick Stack and you will find his books and online videos.

Nightmares

I *wish* this kind of dream did not exist, but it does. Darn it! Most of us call our frightening dreams "nightmares" and they are a pain in the neck, sometimes literally. In a nightmare, we are running away from someone who is trying to kill us; we are on a plane about to crash; we find out that our significant other is having an affair. I think I can speak for all of us when I say that *we all* hate nightmares! When I wake from a nightmare, I am often shaking and my heart is pounding. I have learned over a period of time to tell myself "calm down, it was just a nightmare." The only good thing about a nightmare is the moment when one wakes and feels incredibly relieved that "it was just a dream."

Occasionally nightmares can be empowering. Lately, I have been having nightmares about fighting with a snake, and I am winning the battle. And when someone is trying to attack me, I am scaring the attacker away. When I wake from this kind of dream, I am still shaking but I feel triumphant!

I have been able to reduce the number of nightmares I have by asking the spiritual guidance around me to keep me safe from such negative energies during the night. I listen to spiritual music before sleep and avoid watching or reading about violence of any kind. Scary TV shows before bed can easily create nightmares for me, and I rarely watch anything too scary, no matter what time of day it is. I like to keep up with the news, but sometimes I have to read it on the Internet instead of experiencing the violent film clips on TV. As a psychic, I am more sensitive than many people, and when I watch violence, I feel as if I am right in the middle of it. Do you have similar experiences? I am not advocating that we stop facing the reality of our violent world or try to hide in an ivory tower of meditation. But as extremely sensitive people, we may need to restrict how much violent TV we allow ourselves to watch.

I pray that if my spirit travels during the night, it will go to the realms of the higher energies. These prayers have helped; I have far fewer nightmares.

Become a Dream Detective
Keep a diary of your dreams. Notice the differences in the dreams you have. They may be like mine or entirely different. Do some dreams seem to be teaching you what you need to know while others are trying to process things you may be upset about? As you keep your dream diary, do you notice any patterns? Perhaps you'll notice many of one kind of dream but few of another. And if you decide to open up more fully to your psychic and mediumistic gifts, you may notice your dreams begin to intensify. You may feel as I do: that your spirit is traveling through many universes and learning from those in the world of spirit.

If you have a deep interest in understanding your dreams, discuss them with a teacher or therapist who specializes in dreams. In chapter 4, read more about finding the right helpers: spiritual teachers, groups, and "spirit-friendly" therapists.

Out-of-Body Experiences

Some psychics and mediums have what many call "out-of-body experiences." I have had quite a few of them. The first took place when I was nineteen years old. It is possible that I had earlier experiences when I was asleep or that I do not remember, but in this experience, I was fully awake.

I was living in a dormitory in New York City called the Rehearsal Club. All of the residents were performing artists like me at the time. One day, my roommate and I were talking about psychic experiences and decided to do a psychic experiment. We shrieked with laughter as we started because as far as we were concerned, we were playing a game. We sat near the door to our room and placed a chair at the far end of the room near the window. Our intention was to sit near the door and project our spirits to that chair so our spirits would *meet* on the chair. With a bit of trepidation, I focused on sending my spirit to the chair, and so did my roommate. All of a sudden I felt my spirit fly out of my body and land on that chair, where her spirit was already *there,* waiting for me. It felt to me as if our spirits *flew* to that chair while our physical bodies *remained* near the door. I was astounded and frightened as I wondered if I would have trouble getting my spirit *back* into my physical body. I was aware that the two of us did not know what we were doing, and perhaps I was imagining this whole episode or having a hallucination.

The truth is, I will never know what happened that day. Maybe I did have a hallucination, or maybe I had a genuine out-of-body experience. I was not educated about such matters at that time. What I do know is that I became very frightened of ever trying something like *that* again. My friend and I were *playing* with psychic experience. It was not something we should have been doing without the guidance of a psychic teacher.

I ran away from all that was psychic for about twenty years. It was in the late 1980s that I began to explore my psychic nature again. By that time I was smart enough to know that I needed to find a teacher to study with. I understood that my exploration of the world of spirit was *not* a game and that I shouldn't take the journey by myself. I needed qualified teachers to help me. (Obviously, I did get off that chair and back into my body, as I am here to tell the story.)

Premonitions

Among the most upsetting experiences for newcomers to the psychic realms are premonitions, particularly if they involve a warning that something upsetting may happen. Premonitions that someone will be in an accident or pass on to eternal life (what most people call "dying") can be extremely anxiety-producing. Of all the psychic experiences one can have, a difficult premonition is most likely to make you want to run away from your psychic sensitivity and scream "I do not want to be psychic!" You are not alone if difficult premonitions bother you. Most of the psychics and mediums I know have a hard time with them.

Your Beliefs Regarding Destiny

Your beliefs may impact the way you respond to premonitions. For instance, people who believe that everything in life is pre-destined do not appear to suffer as much when they have premonitions. For these people, having advance notice about what is going to happen and either avoiding it or being prepared for it is just part of the whole scheme of things—for these people, these events were *meant to be*. For instance, clients of mine who are destiny-believers will deeply grieve the death of a younger person, but ultimately they seem to have an acceptance that what happens in life is the will of God. Clients who do not have that belief may have a much more difficult time; some never accept a tragic death. With all due respect to those who believe in destiny, I am simply not in their camp. For me the death of a young person is a complete tragedy and happens not because God destined it, but because we are human beings with physical bodies, and sometimes our bodies become sick or are injured by others. Even though I am a medium, I suspect that if a young loved one of mine died, I would have a very hard time coping.

The subject of destiny is *very* controversial. My objective at the moment is not to try to convince you whether all is destined or not. For our purposes, it does not matter what you believe. What *is* important is exploring *ways to cope* if you are having premonitions. You have to make a choice about "what to do" when you have one!

How to Cope with Premonitions

First, take a deep breath and realize that many people have premonitions. Assess the situation and decide if there is anything you want to *do* as a result of having had this premonition. Your decision may depend on what *kind* of premonition you had.

Simple and enjoyable premonitions:

- I have a feeling that Mary will call me tonight.

- I sense I am going to run into Ron in the next week.

- I think my boyfriend will give me a laptop for my birthday.

Because there is nothing scary about these premonitions, there is no need to take any action at all. Most likely you will enjoy the premonition and then see if you were right. Waiting to find out what happens is fun. If you do get that call from Mary, run into Ron in the supermarket, or get a laptop from your boyfriend, you will be very happy—especially with the laptop!

But what about the scary premonitions:

- I have a feeling that my plane will crash if I fly to Chicago next week.

- I sense that someone in my family is going to die soon.

- I do not think my friend should go hiking tomorrow because something bad is going to happen to her.

Scary premonitions cause most of us to panic. We do not know if the premonitions are real or if we are simply fearful about flying, death, and our friend's safety. What to do? Cancel the trip to Chicago? Fearfully wonder who is going to die? Tell our friend to skip her hike? It is not fun to have these kinds of questions running around your frantic brain. I know—I have experienced terrible anxiety related to premonitions.

I've had years of experience with premonitions, so allow me to share my personal decisions about "what to do." I am not suggesting that you make the same choices I made, but as you read about them, pay attention to your reactions. They will help you get in touch with your own best choices.

Premonitions about Death

I have had premonitions about death. Some turned out to be true; others did not. I did not always realize that I'd had premonitions about the deaths of loved ones until after the passing had taken place. As I looked back, I realized I had been preparing myself and there was a part of me that knew what was going to happen. I have also had very clear premonitions about death, and sometimes my premonitions have been very exact.

However, when I was much younger I had many so-called premonitions that turned out to be *nothing but fear.* I can think of two people who I just *knew* would die before their twenty-fifth birthdays. One is now in her seventies and the other is in his fifties. Those premonitions were not real. They were fearful thoughts that appeared to me as premonitions. Because I had no metaphysical education at that time, I could not evaluate my so-called premonitions. I was frightened. This kind of fearful experience made me want to stop having premonitions and stay away from anything that people called "psychic" or "paranormal." In fact, if I had been better able to deal with these experiences, I might have given in and accepted my psychic nature long before I finally did. If you can benefit from my coping mechanisms, you may not have to run away from your psychic self.

So how do you know if a premonition is authentic? I wish I could tell you, but honestly, *you cannot tell 100 percent of the time if a premonition is real or fear-based.* In my experience, most of the premonitions that are real just drop into my mind; there is little emotion attached. It is as if a message is floating by and my mind just picks it up. Premonitions that turn out to be fears usually come to me when I am in an emotional state.

Premonitions about death cause a terrible dilemma: is there anything you can do to prevent the death? Should you warn someone? What is your responsibility? It's as if burning coals are suddenly placed in your hands and you have to act fast.

I came to the conclusion that the moment of death is between the person who is dying and God. It is not my decision or choice. And it is not my responsibility to tell anyone about my premonition unless there is a very good reason to do so. For instance, if I knew there was something wrong with someone's car and they did not know, I would prevent them from taking a road trip the next day. But this is not a premonition. This is a concern I am having based on the *fact* that this car is not operating properly. If I had a premonition that my friends might be involved in a car crash, I would have to keep my mouth shut and hope that my thoughts were fear-based. I will add that there can be exceptions to this rule. If I had a *very* strong premonition that did not seem fear-based, I would consider sharing it. As you can see, decisions about what to do with scary premonitions are difficult, to say the least!

I prayed for several years for God to stop giving me premonitions about death unless this information was useful to me in some way. If it was important that I knew or that I passed the information to someone else, then I would accept these premonitions from God. Since I have prayed on this, I have not had premonitions about death unless they are useful. For instance, if I am giving a reading and a woman asks if her sick mother will die soon, and I know the client has to travel halfway across the world to see her mother, then I might receive a message from spirit telling me to advise that this woman visit her mother soon, as you never know when she might take a turn for the worst. This is a reasonable and accurate statement. I do *not* state that I sense the mother is going to die soon, because I may be wrong. I feel it is irresponsible to make statements about when someone is going to die, because I have no way of proving to myself that I am having a thought or emotion of my own *or* a true psychic prediction.

Having shared my personal choices with you, let me tell you that some of my colleagues disagree with me. They would tell their clients when they thought one of the client's loved ones was going to die.

Premonitions about Illness

When I have premonitions about the health of another person, I do not share them. It is not my business to diagnose. As with premonitions about death, many psychics and mediums feel it is okay to share their feelings about the health of others. I think is totally irresponsible unless the psychic medium is an experienced medical intuitive who works hand in hand with the medical community so there is a doctor who can *verify* a psychic medium's premonitions about a client's health.

So *what* are you to do if you have visions or premonitions about illness developing in a loved one, friend, or co-worker? In my opinion there is not much you can do unless that person complains of pain or appears significantly unwell. Then encourage that person to get medical help. Even if the person is telling you about his symptoms, you may not want to admit that you had a psychic vision of an illness, because you may scare the person, making him feel worse. Fear will not help. You are better off keeping those psychic visions to yourself and giving the person support.

What if you are giving a reading and have a psychic vision of an illness? This is an important question that those of us who give readings ask ourselves all the time. Should you decide to give readings someday, you will be faced with this dilemma.

When I have visions of illness within the body of a client, I usually silently pray to spirit that the client will mention something about a pain or symptom. It is amazing how the world of spirit helps; usually the client will at some point in our consultation tell me about specific symptoms. She may even ask me if I am picking up on an illness. At that point I tell her that I am not allowed to diagnose and because she is having symptoms, she must see a doctor. It is extremely important that I do not make a big deal of this, because it is so easy for a psychic medium to frighten a client with comments about health. I have to realize that I am not responsible for my client's health. I am not a medical intuitive working closely with a doctor. If I were, I would share more with the client, but medical intuition is a specialty and I would never diagnose unless I had studied with one of the best medical intuitives in the world. Since I have not done that, I have to withhold many of the health visions I have.

Readers Giving Premonitions Often Create Fear

I had a horrible experience when I first sat in a mediumship circle in 1994. A student medium in our spiritual circle told me she could see that a certain kind of disease had developed in my body. I was terrified for years even though I have not had any symptoms of that disease. It was wrong of her to give me a message about my health. The teacher corrected her immediately and reminded her that we are not allowed to diagnose when we give readings.

Another time, an astrologer in India gave me a reading during which he told me when I was going to die and what was going to cause my death. When I waltzed blithely into this reading, which was given in a fancy tourist hotel, I had no idea that I would receive this kind of information. To be honest, the reading freaked me out and still does to this day. Will I psychologically make myself sick at the age of death he specified? Giving this kind of information is not ethical, and there may be no truth to it anyway. As a psychic medium I will not *ever* behave as this reader did.

Perhaps it is good for me to have had these bad experiences. Because I *am* a reader and teacher, these experiences have made it absolutely clear to me that I will not diagnose clients or predict the time of their death or the death of their loved ones. I realize my approach is conservative, but I feel comfortable with these decisions.

As a practicing Spiritualist, I believe that we can receive guidance from spirit for others and ourselves. I also believe that spiritual healing is a positive force and that when used in conjunction with medical care, it can be very effective. We have healing services in our churches. But we never diagnose.

We Do Not Always Know How to React to Premonitions

So far I have not cancelled a trip because of a so-called premonition and I am still here to tell the story. I would not choose to call a friend and tell her to skip her hike because I had a scary premonition about her. Having said this, it is possible that one day I will have a premonition that is so vivid and compelling that I will cancel a trip or try to talk a friend out of doing an activity.

It is only fair to add that sometimes the premonitions we receive *about ourselves* are extremely helpful. For instance, in my younger years I would not pay attention to premonitions that certain people would be dishonest and hurt my feelings. I wanted to see the best in everyone. Over the years, I came to learn that these premonitions (or warnings) should have been heeded. The people my premonitions warned me about turned out to be dishonest and *did* hurt my feelings. As I get older, I pay more attention to the premonitions that relate to me and my well-being. While I realize that a premonition may be incorrect, I no longer dismiss it so easily. I understand a source of wisdom is warning me and knows things that my conscious mind cannot know.

Anything is possible where premonitions are concerned; the bitter truth is that we cannot always feel totally comfortable with what we choose to do with them. Know that as you become more knowledgeable about your psychic and mediumistic gifts, you will become more confident in your ability to make good decisions regarding your premonitions. However, coping with premonitions may never be easy.

Visions of Those Who Have Passed On

Not all psychics have visions of those who have passed on. If your gift is purely psychic, you may have vivid dreams, out-of-body experiences, and premonitions. At times, you may know what others are thinking or feel you receive predictions about the future. If you *also* have visions of people and pets that *have passed on,* then you are having mediumistic experiences as well. My spiritual teachers taught me that all mediums are psychic but not all psychics are mediums. This does not mean that it is any better to be mediumistic. We are not involved in a contest or competition.

I was aware of my psychic gifts for most of my life, but it was not until I was in my forties that I became aware that

I was also a medium. My first vision was of the spirit of my dog who had passed away. The vision looked like the shape of my beloved standard poodle, wrapped in plastic wrap. I didn't just see the image within my mind—I saw it *objectively*. I saw the spirit of my dog move across that room just as I would see a living dog moving, except I knew *this was a vision* because I could see through it.

The second time I had a vision that I could see outside myself (an objective vision), I was with my best girlfriend. I saw a vision of her grandfather standing by the refrigerator in my friend's home. When I described what I had seen and heard, she told me I had given an accurate description of him. I was also able to supply his first name. I was in total shock.

Quite frankly, I did not take my first two visions too seriously. I told myself, "Well, I probably wanted to see the vision of my dog, and perhaps my friend had told me about her grandfather years ago, and suddenly this information that was already in my mind turned into a vision." But these first two visions and those that followed aroused my curiosity enough to motivate me to join a development circle in a Spiritualist church. By then most of the visions I was having were *subjective* visions, within my mind's eye. But the information they contained was just as accurate as in the objective visions of my dog and my friend's grandfather.

And as I sat in circle and had visions of those who had passed on and brought their messages to other members of my circle *whom I knew nothing about,* I realized that these visions were real. At first I thought I must be making lucky guesses, but I reached a tipping point at which I knew that they were not guesses. I told myself if I was *that* good at guessing, I should go to a casino and win millions.

I finally had to admit to myself that there was *no way I could guess so much* about my classmates' loved ones. As other students in the group understood more and more of the evidence I brought them about their loved ones in spirit, I accepted that I was a medium.

How to Evaluate Your Visions

If you are having visions of those who have passed on, the best way to *verify whether these visions are real* is to join a mediumistic development circle. I highly recommend going to the sacred setting of a Spiritualist church. You can also find teachers outside of the religion of Spiritualism who bring a sacred energy to the development of mediumship. You are most likely to find these teachers at spiritual or New Age centers.

If you cannot find a setting where your visions can be verified, it is impossible to know what is really happening. Being with a group of friends who verify your visions is risky because sometimes the members of the group *want* your visions to be real so badly that they accept them too easily. Better to be with a hard-nosed teacher who will only accept good evidence as proof that spirit communication is taking place.

Unexplained Coincidences, Haunted Houses, Spiritual Sites, and Mind-Reading

As psychics, we have so many different kinds of unusual experiences. Not only do we have unexplained coincidences, but we may have stronger reactions to haunted houses and spiritual sites. Add to this list our awareness of the thoughts of others, and it is easy to see that we have a lot to cope with! But with understanding, we *can* cope and we *will* cope.

Unexplained Coincidences

Some coincidences are common and we do not tend to get too excited about them. For instance, say I take a walk in my neighborhood everyday and run into the same neighbor three days in a row, at different times of day. This is coincidental, but not hard to explain. We live in the same neighborhood, we both take walks in that neighborhood, so it is easy to believe we will run into each other occasionally, even three days in a row. Other coincidences are not easy to explain. For sake of discussion, let us call them "unexplained coincidences." Unexplained coincidences can be fun, interesting, comforting, intriguing, and even terrifying. Each of your unexplained coincidences may be different in character.

The most outstanding unexplained coincidence I had was after my father passed to spirit. My dad was my first singing teacher and one day within my mind I heard part of a difficult jazz song he had taught me. A little later that day I heard the same song on the radio in my kitchen. A few hours later I had to take a taxi, and guess what the driver was singing? You guessed it: the same song. Later on that evening I went to a restaurant where a recording of the song was playing. This all happened on the same day, and the song was not a popular one—it was an old song from the 1930s! "Is this the spirit of my father communicating with me?" I wondered. The truth is, there is no way to prove that it was the spirit of my father. I happen to believe it was!

Many of the stories of unexplained coincidences I hear from my clients are hard to explain. From my point of view, it is possible that these clients are having spirit visitations from their loved ones. Their stories involve "signs" such as music, letters or numbers on license plates, birds, pennies, rainbows, and butterflies. I believe that these signs are meant to signal to my clients that the loved ones are present. Often, the signs are given *multiple times* to get the client's attention.

While I suspect that multiple signs are evidence of a spirit visitation, there is no way to prove it beyond a doubt. But if I were receiving multiple signs, I would believe they were from my loved one. I say that so easily today, but it has taken me years to believe the authenticity of these signs. I needed to accumulate years of experiences with my *own* unexplained coincidences and hear the many stories of my students and clients before I could believe that our loved ones communicate with us through signs. I have always been hard to impress, and the world of spirit has had to show me tons of evidence over many years.

It is assuring and rewarding when, during a reading, a communicating spirit is able to verify a client's experience with multiple signs. When the spirit that is using me to communicate with a client tells me about the multiple signs *before* the client has said anything about the signs she is receiving, I am convinced that I am getting this information *from the spirit* and not from the client.

Scary Unexplained Signs

I have a hard time when a client calls and says something like "It has rained every Tuesday afternoon for the past three weeks and I sense that this means I should not drive on Tuesdays or I may have an accident. What do you think, Carole Lynne?" For me, this client is taking a coincidence and turning it into a superstitious experience.

Another example: a client tells me she regularly dreams that something terrible is going to happen to her. She wonders whether she is simply experiencing her fear through her dreams or if a spirit is trying to give her a warning she should pay attention to. Personally, I would go crazy if I thought all bad dreams were warnings. Most of us have bad dreams occasionally, and some of us have the same bad dreams over and over. There is no way to absolutely prove what these dreams mean, despite all the books on dream symbology.

Each one of us has a choice as we try to come to an understanding of our recurring bad dreams. I know someone who stays in the house all of the time because of her constant bad dreams about going out. I, on the other hand, am more comfortable arriving at the conclusion that I just *do not know* what these dreams mean. I am going to go about my life as usual. I am more likely to pay attention to warnings I feel are from my *"inner guidance"* than I am to warnings from bad dreams. Having said that, there is always the chance that I will have an exceptional experience that will cause me to respond differently. If my inner guidance tells me to pay attention to a bad dream because it is really a warning, then I will pay attention.

Haunted Houses and Sacred Sites

I sometimes wonder whether the thousands of people who visit "haunted" sites are actually creating the energy that pervades such places. I am quite opinionated on the subject of haunted sites and will cut to the chase and tell you: do not go there! If you want to attract a lot of negative energy just for the thrill of it, be my guest. But for those of you who want to lead a calmer, less sensational life, stay away from the for-profit commercial places labeled "haunted." I make an exception on Halloween and visit neighbors who make their houses look scary for the holiday. But I do not visit for-profit haunted places, ever.

When hundreds of people gather at a site where they expect to see a ghost, and they focus on these scary feelings, accentuating the experience with an occasional scream or two, are they responsible for creating an energetic vibration that remains in the walls of that house? If so, that house will feel more haunted each week as hundreds of tourists leave imprints of their spooky feelings there. Perhaps *originally* there was a spirit who caused some trouble there, and when someone decided to make it a tourist site, the people who visited kept *adding* to this spooky energy with their own vibrations. My fantasy is that some perfectly well-adjusted spirits stop by the "haunted" site, look at the tourists gathered there, and say to each other, "My, my, these people are seeing things and saying we have done things that we would *never* do! We don't screech like that."

Keep in mind that a house that is said to have spirits in it is *not necessarily* creepy or haunted. I had a spirit in my house at once, but I was not afraid and I did not consider my house to be haunted. I have been to houses occupied by spirits who need help leaving the house to go towards the light of the Eternal Life. I do not think of these houses as haunted, and I have no problem with visiting them. But I do not go to houses that are trying hard to be scary in order to attract customers. These houses may attract spirits that I do not feel like hanging out with.

Sacred Sites

Among my favorite sacred sites are the Notre Dame Cathedral in Paris, the Matrimandir (Temple of the Mother) in Auroville, India, and the Holy Rosary Church in Makawao, Hawaii. These sacred sites and others like them may have become more sacred because of the *thoughts and prayers* of those who visit them. *Originally* an extremely advanced spiritual person may have visited a site, and then over the years thousands of people came from all over the world to pray. As the prayers were offered, the site *became* more holy. The prayers of the visitors are blended together into a beautiful and sacred energy that one can feel the moment one enters the site.

Visit the Sacred, Dodge the Spooky

Some people love anything spooky—the scarier the better. If that is what attracts you, then you will look for a teacher who thrives on sensationalism. However, I think becoming involved in the *sacred* aspects of spirit communication is a lot healthier. Your energy will vibrate at a much more spiritual level, therefore drawing higher spiritual energies to you.

I've never had any problems with so-called negative or evil spirits. I wonder if life as a psychic and medium would be different for me if I was drawn to the sensationalism of haunted places. Think of the expression "like attracts like." As you make choices about who to study with and which spiritual circle or class to sit with, consider: wouldn't you prefer to hang out with the more *spiritual* spirits?

In fairness to those psychics and mediums who work in so-called haunted houses: there are many who feel it is important to investigate these houses to research the phenomena that occur there. This is important work; sometimes a location is called "historical" rather than "haunted." I am comfortable visiting historical houses to seek out spirits who can give me messages about the history of the location. I prefer to call these houses "spirit-occupied" rather than "haunted."

If you do not stay away from sensational and spooky places, do not blame me if you get yourself into psychological trouble. If you are more sensitive to the energies around you than the average person, you need to stay away from spooky places and people. Let those who are less sensitive have fun at haunted houses.

FYI: My grandkids may think I am a bore and a bit stodgy. When they ask me about ghosts, I tell them that ghosts are beautiful spirits dressed up in their Halloween costumes. They are having a fun evening called Halloween and they are not really scary. A six-year-old who wants to scream and have a scary time may find me to be not only old but also old-fashioned. So be it!

Mind-Reading

I first heard about ESP, or extra-sensory perception, in the 1950s. ESPs are perceptions that we do not receive from the so-called "normal" five senses: sight, smell, hearing, touch, and taste. When I noticed, at around age thirteen, that I was reading the minds of some of my friends, I called it ESP. More often these days, at least outside the scientific community, ESP is called *psychic communication.* I assume most scientists still prefer to use the term ESP in their scientific studies about these phenomena—the word "psychic" can still raise eyebrows in the halls of science.

Many of us who are psychic have experiences in which we feel we are picking up on the thoughts of others. We will think about a certain subject and suddenly the person we are with will start talking about the same subject. In this case, we may have *heard within our minds* the thoughts of the other person just before the person began to speak. If we have this kind of experience regularly, we begin to understand that we have psychic abilities.

On the subject of ESP ethics: I think it is wrong to attempt to pick up on the thoughts of others unless they have scheduled an intuitive reading with me. I am not interested in prying into the thoughts of those around me. If I pick up their thoughts without trying, however, I do not blame myself.

Where Do You Go from Here?

Okay, so you are not imagining that you are psychic! Where do you go from here?

We've looked at some of the psychic and mediumistic experiences many of us have had. If your experiences have been troubling you, I hope this chapter put you at ease. Always remember that while it is important for you to understand and own whatever psychic and mediumistic experiences you have, *it is your choice as to what you do with these spiritual gifts.* You do not have to develop your gifts unless you feel *compelled and called* to do so. Some of you may not wish to verify your experiences or do anything to develop this aspect of yourself. I know many who have had incredible visions of their loved ones and have absolutely no desire to become mediums for the purpose of communicating with the spirits of *other* people's loved ones. They are grateful for the visitations from their *own* loved ones. Many people with this attitude do not have visions that extend beyond their own loved ones.

Those who have *many* visions of spirits—not only their own loved ones, but the loved ones of people they do not know—have a harder time deciding "what to do" with this spiritual gift! If you are having many visions, my advice is to take these first experiences in stride. Take a *"let's wait and see what happens"* attitude. The truth is, you may be in a phase of your life where you will have visions of spirits, and this phase may or may not last. If these visions continue for over a year, *then* make a decision about whether to find a psychic or mediumship teacher. *Again, you are in charge of your life.* You have options even when spirits are trying to communicate with you or through you. *You do not have to listen to spirits just because they are spirits any more than you would have to allow strangers to come up to you on the street and monopolize your time with chatter.*

What if you happen to be a scientist on the verge of a breakthrough? Do you really want to distract yourself by going to a psychic or mediumistic development group? Or what if you are a busy parent who is not comfortable exploring spirit communication around your kids, and on top of that you are part of a religion that will not tolerate your studying anything psychic or mediumistic? Many people who have spiritual gifts are simply not living a lifestyle that allows them to develop their gifts comfortably. Be honest with yourself about what will make you most comfortable as you incorporate your spiritual gifts into your life.

Each Question Leads to Another Question

As we explore whether there is proof of psychic and mediumistic experience, many questions emerge. We cannot scientifically prove that these experiences are "real," which leaves us open to insults like "quack" and "fraud." In our defense, let me say that scientists want psychics and mediums to be able to bring repeatable experiences on demand. This is not possible. What spirit is going to communicate through the exact same medium to the exact same client and say the same things said in five previous readings?

At this point in history, I feel we have enough evidence to prove that *we do communicate* with those in spirit. Mediums have been able to present so much evidence about those who have passed on—evidence of which they had no prior knowledge. We can't simply chalk this knowledge up to good guesses. But we do not yet have the scientific instruments to prove *how* this takes place. There remain many unanswered questions about spiritual experience and spirit communication.

I feel it is more responsible to be open about what we know for sure, and what still needs to be proved. This approach does not make me look as smart as I could look if I made sweeping claims about spiritual experiences, but I feel comfortable with my approach. *I absolutely believe and know that the spiritual experiences I have had are real,* but in some cases, I have to acknowledge that I base my beliefs on my own numerous experiences. I cannot state them as scientific fact.

Intellect and Intuition

Many highly spiritual people do not believe that intellect is the highest authority. They believe that Truth is beyond what the intellect can understand, and put spiritual experience and intuition above intellectual discovery. For many of us raised in the Western world, it is hard to get our heads around this idea. However, those of us who are experienced psychics and mediums have had experiences that have proven to us that there is a lot to learn if we allow ourselves to go deep within and receive guidance from a Source that cannot be proven by science.

My goal is not to convert you into any particular way of thinking. My hope is that you can find a way to be comfortable with the gifts you have received, and make choices about how you want to use or subdue them. When you accept your abilities and make choices about how to use or not use them, you will live a more balanced and emotionally healthy life. If you choose to share your gifts with others, that is a good choice. If you are more interested in doing other things with your life, that choice is just as good.

I wish I could put all our psychic and mediumistic experiences into a box, wrap it, tie it up neatly in a bow. Our mission would be accomplished; we would understand everything (or at least think we did). I wish I could sound smarter by saying we can understand all spiritual experience. On the intellectual level, there will always be experiences we do not understand, and we will struggle to arrive at the Truth.

However, if we develop a strong connection with the Divine so that we can experience a Knowing Within, we will find the ultimate Truth. There is a spark of Divinity within each of us. This spark is our connection to the Divine. As we grow and develop spiritually, we will understand on a deeper, non-verbal level.

TWO

Take Special Care of Your Psychic Self

Psychics are more sensitive than average people. We need to manage our schedules so that we have enough time to take care of ourselves. We need to do whatever it takes to stay physically and emotionally healthy!

Avoid the Fast Track

Want to take the fast track to God? Want to be enlightened over a long weekend? Beware of fast track spiritual seminars and instant-magic teachers. If you eat fast food, you eat junk. If you seek fast spiritual transformation, you will only skim the surface of the spiritual energy that is available within you. Better to have the patience to take a longer and deeper look. Take the spirituality fast track and you will find a junk God. Walk the path of patience and you will find peace, happiness, and success.

Forget about attending weekend seminars in hotel ballrooms or on beautiful mountain tops, where you receive initiations that promise to instantly transform you. Yes, you will be transformed into a high-flying emotionally heightened nutcase, but when you crash a week later, you will realize that these initiations that you earned so quickly are not worth the certificates they are printed on. You will be wondering why you feel so terrible and yet you will already be looking for the next quick-fix seminar to make you into an "enlightened pseudo-avatar." *Get used to the idea that there is no quick fix in spiritual development.* Taking care of yourself as you develop spiritually is a lifetime process; for those who believe in reincarnation, it is a process that extends over many lifetimes. If you want to walk the spiritual path, pray for sincerity and patience. Those who want instant transformation often end up crashing emotionally. You can *avoid all that* by slowing down, looking deep within, and not allowing yourself to be grasped by some commercial guru who is looking for disciples.

In chapter 1 you read about many kinds of psychic and mediumistic experiences. Could you relate to some of them? If you can, then you no longer have to ask yourself if *you are psychic or making it up.* Of course you will always have to look at *each* experience you have with the eye of a spiritual detective in order to determine which experiences are authentically psychic or mediumistic. But this task comes with the territory. Being a healthy skeptic about your own experiences will never lead you in the wrong direction. This will prevent you from being so enamored of your experiences that you blow them way out of proportion and end up with a list of exaggerated stories and an ego inflated large enough to fill a hotel ballroom. On the other hand, never let the skeptical side of yourself talk you out of accepting an authentic psychic or mediumistic experience. Understanding our psychic selves is a balancing act!

When you accept that you are a psychic and/or medium, you have a responsibility to take extra good care of yourself. Have you noticed that you are more sensitive than the average person? Being extra sensitive demands extra self-care. This takes effort, discipline, and commitment. Ouch! I realize that is a lot for us to demand of ourselves, but it is necessary in order for us to live healthy, balanced lives.

Evaluate Your Physical, Mental, Emotional, and Spiritual Health

You may find that you are more sensitive to food than many of your friends. When you go into huge retail stores, you may tire easily. Smells may bother you more than they affect others. Perhaps you're starting to think you are an over-sensitive hypochondriac, and for some of you this could be true. But most of you are not overly anything: you are just *very* sensitive. Someday you'll accept this blessing. You'll come to understand that it is your extreme sensitivity that makes it possible for you to communicate with the spirits of other living people and with those in spirit who have passed on into eternal life. It is your sensitivity that allows you to communicate with higher minds and spiritual presences. Unfortunately, there is often a price to pay for these gifts—it is not always so easy for the extremely sensitive person to get along in life. But it can be done, I promise!

For years, I thought there was something really wrong with me. I was only in my thirties—why couldn't I sit in a rock concert for four hours? Why couldn't I eat three pieces of pizza and drink beer and not feel sick and exhausted the next day? Why couldn't I party all weekend? When I did any of those things too often, I felt sick for days. I wondered why I was such a wimp, such a baby.

In mid-life, when I realized I could communicate with spirit, I had the privilege of having a fabulous teacher take me under her wing. She taught me that as I opened up to the world of spirit, I would become extremely sensitive. By this time I was not only dealing with all my own thoughts and feelings, but picking up on the thoughts and feelings of others, as well as receiving messages from those in spirit. That was a lot to cope with. In addition, my teacher told me that I would be more open to the "influence of various energies" created by various people—including energies that had a life of their own. (We will look at the "influences" later in this chapter.) At times I would feel irritable and unable to control my emotions until I adjusted to the new energies that were coming to me. To be honest, I did not believe what my teacher was telling me—I did not want to. I could not cope with the idea of becoming even more sensitive each year. But my teacher was right. My sensitivity kept increasing and I had to work hard to learn how to cope with myself. But I *have* coped, thank you very much!

I have always been psychic, but I was in my forties and fifties when I began to see the spirits of those who had passed on. My sensitivity grew and grew. I came to understand that I needed to *manage my sensitivity* and take care of myself in a very special way, *whether others understood me or not.* After learning how to manage all the aspects of myself, I needed to learn how to manage the others in my life who were totally skeptical about what I was experiencing. I found I could get support from others if I had patience and compassion for their skepticism. It was not necessary for me to isolate myself and only associate with extra-sensitive people like myself. I found I could have a variety of people in my life.

Accept yourself. If you are like me and need an unusually healthy diet, lots of sleep, and limited visits to crowded places, so be it. These adjustments are not necessary for all sensitive people, but for many of us they are essential.

Your Physical Health

It has been said that the body is the temple of the soul, or the clothing the soul wears while it is living a human life. As a psychic and/or mediumistic person, you have more awareness than the average person. Your body picks up on vibrations from other people, animals, and events that are happening in the world. In order to assimilate all this energy, you need to be as healthy as possible. Many spiritual teachers call taking care of themselves "becoming a pure channel for spirit." I find that when I take care of my body, I am better able to handle my psychic and mediumistic experiences. Of course everyone, psychic or not, needs to care for his or her body, but I perceive that psychic people need to work even harder at self-care.

When you look at your body, what do you see? Take a really good look at your body, just as you would look at your car, and ask yourself, "What shape is this body in? What kind of maintenance does it require in order to get the most years of use?" When you bring your car to the shop and hear the mechanic's diagnosis, you are able to accept that you need new brake pads or tires. You know if you don't maintain your car, you might get into an accident, or your car might die on you. Same with your body: look at your body and see what kind of maintenance is required. Maintain your body properly and it will run smoothly. You will get more years out of it than you would if you stuck your head in the sand and refused to do the required body maintenance.

Many of us want to eat, drink, and smoke whatever we want while we lounge in front of the TV or cruise around the Internet. Some people get away with this behavior and live to be ninety-five, while others do everything right and still get serious diseases when they're young. Fortune aside, many of us cut our lives short due to our lifestyles. "But I can't give up eating bags of corn chips in front of the TV," we cry. "I work hard and that is my only enjoyment in life." Even pious vegans find themselves eating too many sweets, however vegan those sweets may be, and end up with the same pot bellies as the heavy beer drinkers. This is a great time for a physical exam to find out if there are areas of your health that need more attention.

Mental/Emotional Health

Extra sensitive people like us are often on emotional over-drive because of all the energies we are picking up on. As has been stated, we are not only experiencing our own feelings, but picking up on the feelings of others. We need to learn to sense when it is our *own* feeling we are reacting to, and when we are taking on the emotion of *another person* or *group*. Additionally, we need to learn how to sense when a thought or feeling is a *message from the spirit* of one who has passed on, or a message from what I call *"Guidance"* and what many call their spirit guides, God, or the Divine.

Sometimes when I start to get emotionally exhausted, irritable, and cranky, I ask myself, "What am I reacting to? Is this upset feeling the result of something that really bothers me, or am I experiencing the distress of someone I love?"

If I come to the conclusion that the upset is mine, then I need to do whatever I can to improve the situation. I need to ask myself, "What is this thought or feeling trying to tell me? What information can I get from this bubble of irritable energy?" If I am feeling bad about myself and am willing to look at the message coming to me from that feeling, I can get good suggestions about what to do. If I have been eating too much, that's my irritability warning me to stop overeating and get back on my healthy diet. If I am feeling bad because someone did a better job than I did, I need to tell my ego to stop being so jealous.

Once my irritable energy has given me the feedback I need, I can simply let go of these irritable thoughts and replace them with happier and more positive ones. If this approach does not work, I can listen to beautiful music (ahhhhhhh, such a great mood changer) or do some light exercise. There are dresser drawers that need cleaning. I can find something productive to do instead of holding on to my bad mood. It is up to me! And of course, it is up to you, too.

If I decide that I am not reacting to my own thoughts, but *picking up* on the upset feeling of a loved one, then I need to *step back emotionally;* my taking on another person's emotional pain does not do anyone any good. I can be more helpful by looking at my loved one's problem from an objective point of view. Maybe I can make suggestions, or perhaps it will be more helpful to simply listen compassionately.

What thoughts are you filling your mind with? While we are used to thinking about what we put in our stomachs, it is not as easy for us to think about what we put in our minds. In fact, many people do not feel they have control over their thoughts. It is easier to give up ice cream than it is to give up negative or depressing thoughts. We act as if our thoughts just come to us and we *have* to accept them. After all, we cry, "this is what I am *feeling.*" A thought can grow into a powerful emotion such as anger, jealousy, or sadness. Sometimes we become controlled by these thoughts and emerging feelings. Of course we do not want to suppress them, but we do not need to let these thoughts and feelings overpower us and run our lives. We can choose what thoughts we allow to take up our mental space.

I am not a therapist, but I notice that with the increasing popularity of cognitive therapy and behavioral therapy, more and more friends and clients are working at having greater control over their thoughts. It is important to add that if you have deep emotional problems and persistent negative thoughts that you cannot get rid of, seek professional help from a qualified therapist. Learn how to find a "spirit-friendly" therapist in chapter 4.

What Is an Influence?

As we strive to take care of our mental and emotional health, one of our challenges is becoming aware of what I am naming "influences." As "influences" are not easy to identify, it is important that we take the time to define them as well as possible.

I have met many people who, when they describe something that makes them feel uncomfortable or frightened, use terms such as evil spirits, negative energies, negative vibes, horrible vibes, and frightening vibrations. Usually these terms are used when talking about a place, a person, or a group of people. "There is an evil spirit in that house." "That woman gives off negative vibes." "I don't like the energy in that store."

What are we really talking about when we use these expressions? How can we quantify what a negative vibe or energy *is*? It is easier for us to conceive of what we call an "evil spirit" because we are able to create an *image* of a spirit in the form of someone who once lived a human life. But when it comes to talking about negative vibrations and energies, what images do we have in our minds? We cannot prove that negative energies exist any more than we can prove that sacred energies exist. But we *know* that both negative and sacred vibrations fill our world—we feel these energies all the time. And as psychics, we may feel energies or "influences" more often than the average person.

Here is an example of an influence. You are walking through a haunted house. You find that the "atmosphere" feels different than that of a sacred temple of worship. You agree that the vibes are negative. One person in your group starts to shake and insists that an evil spirit has taken hold of him. The rest of you do not see anything like that happening.

Many times when I hear people insist that they have become possessed by so-called evil spirits, I wonder if what these people are really reacting to is the *influence of a vibration* that is *in* that location, *not* the individual spirit of someone who has passed on. When people get into a frenzy about the "evil spirits that are lurking around," I feel they are reacting to thoughts or behaviors of their own, of those around them, *or of influences that they have come into contact with in the location.* More often than not, I come to the conclusion that it is *not an evil spirit* causing the commotion. Believe me, if there was a genuine evil spirit present, it would prove its existence—we'd see objects flying through the air and hear phantom sounds. But when someone simply has a creepy feeling and declares he is possessed by a spirit, I am not impressed.

Here is another example: You visit a location where violence has taken place during a war and experience the violent vibrations of the past. One could say that as tourists we *expect* to feel these vibrations, and therefore we are making it up when we say a place has negative vibes. In some cases this is true: the visitors may be creating the negative vibes.

However, a number of times I have visited a location *without knowing* that anything violent happened there, and immediately felt such negative vibrations that I needed to leave the location—only to find out later that people had been tortured and killed there. I feel that the violent actions of the past left what many call "an energetic imprint" in that location. For the sake of this discussion, let us say that the violence created vibrations that when attached to each other formed into many "bubbles of energy" that adhered to the walls of the location. I have had these experiences in more than one location: at a castle and at a historic public bath house in Europe. I have heard similar stories from my mediumistic friends, my students, and my clients. Perhaps you have had a similar experience. I do not wish to name the specific places where I have sensed these negative vibrations, as this will only attract people to those sites who are looking for scary experiences.

My question is this: If vibrations can create bubbles of energy that can attach to the walls in a location, what is to prevent some of these bubbles of energy from floating out the door and moving on down to the road to who knows where?

My personal experiences as a psychic tell me that what many call negative force fields, evil spirits, and the like are really these bubbles of negative energy that are everywhere in our world and perhaps in the universe. I perceive that positive experiences also create positive energies that group together in bubbles and travel throughout our world and universe. In my psychic perception, often when we speak about reacting to the "vibes" of a person or place, we are reacting to the bubbles of energy that are around us at that moment. These energies may feel negative or positive.

As extra-sensitive people, it is important to know that when we have a thought or feeling that does not seem to come from inside us, from another person, or from the spirit of someone who has passed on, we may be reacting to a bubble of positive or negative energy. For the purposes of this discussion, I will call these "influences." If my perception is correct, then as we discuss the many things we may be reacting to as psychics, we have to include "influences" on our list. You may find it helpful to make a copy of this list and carry it with you. When you are feeling overwhelmed with thoughts and feelings, take a look at your list and try to identify where they are coming from. Is a particular thought or feeling created by one of the following?

- A thought of your own

- A thought of another human being

- A message from the spirit of one who has passed on

- A message from a higher source of guidance

- An influence that is creating an emotional environment

Warning: While this list may be helpful, do not allow yourself to become compulsive about using it. When you are overwhelmed with thoughts and feelings, it may be more helpful to let go of whatever is on your mind and do something relaxing, like listening to your favorite music.

Fear

We may come into contact with several types of "influences." The first is the influence of fear. Following is a story of an experience I had in my twenties when it was very difficult for me to tell the difference between a message from my Guidance and the influence of fear.

I began to have thoughts that warned me against taking airplanes. One day I had an extremely intense and specific thought that if my dad took his scheduled flight from New York to California the next day, his plane would crash and he would die. I spent a full day struggling to decide whether to call my Dad and tell him. I wasn't sure if I was having an authentic psychic premonition or being influenced by fear. I decided not to call my father. I reasoned that if I called him, I would forever have to alert people when I had a feeling something bad was going to happen to them. I did not want that responsibility, especially because I was not sure if the fearful thought I was having was correct. The next day my dad got on the plane to California and arrived safe and sound!

What I learned from this and other similar experiences is that sometimes what I am hearing is *not* a psychic message from a higher source of wisdom. Instead, I have either created this fear from my own thoughts and feelings or those of someone around me, or I have picked up on the *free-floating influence of fear.* As I look back on this experience, I wonder if I picked up on fearful energy in New York City, where I lived. Or had I been watching violent TV shows or movies? Did something separate from my own thoughts connect me with the vibrations of fear?

The *influence of fear* can create all kinds of drama within an individual. My intense anxiety that my dad would die taught me a great lesson: not all the fearful reactions I have are from a source of greater wisdom. Perhaps I did not want my father to go out of town and instead of getting in touch with my feeling of sadness, my mind found a great opportunity to *create fear* about his trip. Or perhaps I had been in an environment where I picked up on the influence of fear and *under that influence* I became filled with fear. It was definitely not a message from a source of wisdom giving a credible warning, because my dad took the trip and arrived safely.

Our discussion of influences could fill several books. But for our purposes, let us look at two more influences: the influence of logic and reason, and the influence of charismatic charm.

Logic and Reason

Let me state emphatically that in order for human beings to lead organized and sensible lives, we need to be logical and reasonable. Logic and reason are our best friends! But like most things, there is a downside. Let us look at ways the *influence of logic and reason* may get in the way of our spiritual development.

When we are having mystical experiences and start to hear authentic messages from higher sources of wisdom, *the influence of logic and reason* can spoil our otherwise ethereal experience. This influence does *not* want to have anything to do with mystical experiences. After all, it has its own set of protocols, and sometimes-rigid rules imposed by science, society, religious and political beliefs, and old adages passed down through the family. It will do anything in its power to *stop* the mystical experience. It starts throwing balls of reason at you like a baseball pitcher out of control—it throws *so* much caution in your face that you may never have a chance to experience the truly mystical spiritual occurrence.

Do Not Allow an Influence of Logic and Reason to Block Positive Mystical Experiences

When I have mystical experiences, I am in touch with my inner self. The part of me that is able to receive Divine messages is open and receptive. I feel calm, peaceful, and very positive. I do not want to allow the influence of logic and reason to talk me out of allowing myself to have this connection with a higher source of wisdom.

What most helped me to *accept* mystical experience was to have my messages from the spirits of those who had passed on validated. This validation proved to me that there really *was* a world of spirit out there. Because I am a very logical and (hopefully) reasonable person, I could not have accepted the mystical part of myself if I had not trained as a psychic and medium. During this training I gave many readings, and when those I read for *verified the information I brought and understood the messages, I knew I was not making it up.* Some of you may not need this kind of verification, but I did. This validation proved to me once and for all that there is an afterlife, a world of spirit out there, and that we can communicate with the individual spirits of those who have passed on. And as my Guidance gave me more messages that were truly helpful to me in my life, I began to accept that there is a spark of Divinity within each of us that is able to connect with the God of our understanding.

I would not have been able to continue my spiritual development if I had not received the validation I needed. The *best thing* I did was join a spiritual development circle in a Spiritualist church. If you want to understand your spiritual gifts, train with a good teacher—one who is a Spiritualist or who is associated with a spiritual or New Age center.

The Influence of Charismatic Charm

This influence can get us into a lot of trouble if we do not *recognize* its mischievous and sensational ways. When you are drawn to a person, no matter how much of a loser or liar this person may be, you may be under the *influence of charismatic charm* that is starting to exert its power over you. This charismatic charm often creates feelings of sexual attraction or a magnetic pull to a so-called spiritual leader or Hollywood guru. When an individual is under the influence of this vibration, he or she absolutely knows that the person he or she is attracted to is the one and only soul mate—even if the person is married with five kids, or a drug dealer. This influence draws people to spiritual teachers looking for students to dominate. It attracts people into bad relationships or cult-like spiritual communities. This is a very dangerous influence—it can easily draw our attention.

As we conclude the discussion of influences, let us remember that when we have thoughts and feelings that do not seem to be coming from us or someone near us, we should be skeptical and consider whether an influence is responsible.

Three Things to Remember

1. Authentic spiritual messages come to us in a calm and loving manner. Our psychic and mediumistic nature is our connection to the Divine. As we learn to listen to this voice, we find that

the Divine Consciousness has an effect on our day-to-day consciousness. We may feel more stable and peaceful. Over a period of time I have noticed that the fearful thoughts I have when I am affected by the influence of fear are dramatic! Messages that come to me from my Guidance contain no passion: just news and guidance.

2. You do not have to be a victim of any negative influence. In fact, as a person with psychic experience, you may be more capable of getting in touch with the negative influences around you, and you may hold a more effective psychic warning system that will guide you when you feel affected by negative influences.

3. The names of the influences in this chapter are labels I have created in order to discuss the different free-floating vibrations that may affect our thoughts and feelings. When we are under these influences, we are not receiving spiritual messages.

Sacred Spiritual Influences

It is my personal belief that a power greater than any human being sends us important warnings. Once, while I was driving, a message from spirit told me to slow down and get over to the side of the road. Paying attention to this warning saved my life—soon after, a truck ran through a red light. Had I not slowed down, I would not be here to tell the story. My life has been saved many times by these warnings. I have also received cautions about particular people who have come into my life. I have steered clear of these people, no matter how charismatic, and in time I have seen events unfold that have proven that the spiritual warning I received was right on target. Some people might call what I am describing "an intuitive hit" or a "correct gut reaction." Unlike my fearful thoughts about my dad's airplane flight, these messages came to me *without drama and emotion*: just as simple but direct warnings.

Don't Become an Energy Freak

As you spend your time around people and places that have spiritual energy, you may notice how much better you feel. Stay away from the negative when you can. *However,* I am not suggesting that you become what I call an "energy freak" or part of the "energy police." People who get caught up in inspecting every person, place, and thing to determine the quality of the energy can become obsessive about it. *That* is not healthy!

Take care of your mental and emotional self by living the highest quality of life possible without becoming overly self-conscious about the energy you are within at a particular moment.

The Spiritual and Transcendent

In addition to taking special care of your body and mind, you need to feed yourself spiritually. If you are a member of a religion that would not approve of your psychic or mediumistic nature, I have compassion for you. You may be conflicted about whether to stay in your religion. Do *not* immediately run from the religion you have been part of for so long. This religion has given you your spiritual roots. Take your time—you may find a way to open up to your psychic and mediumistic gifts *and* stay in your religion. And some of you may decide not to develop your gifts because it will create too much of a conflict with the beliefs of a religion you treasure and love.

After a long period of consideration, I did chose to leave my former religion and become a Spiritualist because I needed my religion to honor spirit communication. But many psychic and mediumistic people visit Spiritualist churches and do not become members. "Don't tell anyone I was here," they tell me. Some of them even attend classes that are open to the public, which most Spiritualist churches offer.

Perhaps organized religion is not for you at all, and you are more comfortable being part of a spiritual circle that meets in a New Age bookstore or spiritual center. Whatever you choose, it is good for you to be around others who are having the same psychic and mediumistic experiences. Being connected to a spiritual group is a way to be reminded regularly that spirit communication is a *sacred practice:* it is *not* sensational and it is *not* a party game!

Give Yourself Alone Time

While it is important to have time with others who have experiences similar to yours, it is just as important for us extra-sensitive people to have time alone. We tend to get over-stimulated, and we need to be in environments without much stimulation.

A spiritual day for me is a day alone. I can walk outside and see the beauty of this earth. I can read spiritual literature and listen to whatever music I wish. I can meditate.

At moments I can pray and listen to the messages I receive from the God of my understanding.

Take Extra Special Care of Your Psychic Self

You are in charge of your life. The God of your understanding is here to guide you. If you have received the gifts of being psychic and mediumistic, accept them with gratitude. Realize that while you are different, you still have many things in common with those who are not psychic.

Take the self-care recommended in this chapter seriously. Your body, mind, and spirit need extra-special care. Take care of your body by carefully selecting the food you eat. Make sure your diet is nutritious. See your doctor and find out what kind of exercise is best for you. And schedule periods of relaxation each week so that you are able to sleep at night. If you have trouble sleeping, get medical help. Remember that your body is the temple of your spirit. Take care of it!

It is equally important to take care of your mind. Remember that because you are extra-sensitive and pick up on many of the thoughts and feelings of others, you need to have time to sort out which thoughts and feelings are yours and when you are falling under the influence of another person. If need be, find a "spirit-friendly therapist."

Take care of your spirit in the way that works best for you. Some may attend a house of worship; others may find walks in the park the best way to feed themselves spiritually. As you open up to the spirit within, the part of you many call "the higher self," you may find that you are receiving more guidance. Learn to *evaluate* when you are receiving guidance from the God of your understanding. With time and patience, you may discover, as I have, that when God brings guidance, the quality of the experience is totally different from the experience of "thinking." The guidance brings with it a very special and sacred energy.

THREE

Managing Your Relationships with Others

THE GOOD NEWS IS that you can learn to communicate
with others about your psychic self, and while not everyone
will believe you, many will support you as you explore and
expand your spiritual gifts. *Of course* some people will not
believe you! Despite what some of your friends and loved
ones may think of you, you do *not* have two heads. But you
do have two sets of eyes: your physical eyes, and what I call
the "spiritual eyes within." These eyes allow you to "see"
things you have never seen before—like visions of those
who have passed on.

The world you and I "see" with our "spiritual eyes" is
often called "the unseen world" within our psychic community, simply because *most outside our community do
not see it.* For us, this so-called "unseen world" becomes
more "seen" each day as we have dreams, waking visions,

premonitions, and messages from the guidance within us. Yet in our skeptical world, many of the people we love and care about do *not* have the same experiences we have; for them, this new world we are "seeing" *does not exist.* You and I are experiencing a world with two levels: a level seen by everyone, including our skeptical loved ones; and this psychic level that is seen by a select few. (When I talk about "seeing" I also include spiritual hearing and sensing—I use the word "seeing" in an inclusive manner.) When you talk about what you "see" with a loved one who does not "see" in the same way, you might as well be telling your loved one that our planet co-exists with another planet that only some people can see. Sounds like science fiction, doesn't it? This creates quite a communication gap, to say the least!

Would *you* believe it? Can you blame the skeptics you love so dearly for not believing you? If you had not had the experiences you've had, would you believe a friend who came to you and said, "I had the most amazing vision the other day. I saw an image of my aunt, who died five years ago. She was standing next to the stove, wearing a pink dress"? Most likely you would suspect that your friend was imagining the whole incident because she missed her aunt.

Why would you expect non-psychic people to believe you? A person with no experience simply cannot grasp your vivid dreams, premonitions, and visions. What you are saying sounds totally unbelievable, and you can't fault them for being skeptical. They do not have a basis of experience on which they can stand in order *to* believe you.

If the non-believer is polite, you will most likely hear an uncomfortable statement like "that is very interesting." The use of the word "interesting" is sometimes a clue to me that a person does not want to offend me, but does not really want to hear any more about my experiences either. When I hear this word, I gradually and politely move towards another topic of conversation (unless I am speaking with a close loved one, and need to talk about my psychic experiences no matter how negative a vibe I may be feeling).

Sometimes Skeptics Hurt Our Feelings

Of course we are sad when loved ones do not believe what we are seeing. We want to share *everything* with our significant others, family, and friends. Talking to them can be challenging, but if you have patience, *it IS possible to communicate about yourself in a way that will encourage others to support you, even if they do not believe you.* Some of us are fortunate enough to have loved ones who are also psychic or simply intrigued by psychic phenomena. More often than not, a good number of loved ones do *not* understand. We need to work *with* them to receive their support.

Difficult Remarks

Your acquaintances and loved ones may hurl offensive remarks at you. Some of the questions I've heard over the years include:

- You never saw spirits before. I have known you for years. What has happened to you? Get a grip!

- Who have you been hanging out with? Who has talked you into all this nonsense?

- You are *not* the same person I met. I don't know if I can handle these stories about reading people's minds and seeing things. It scares me.

- What would your mother say if she knew about *this*?

- Have you been reading too much science fiction lately? What has gotten into you?

- Yes, that is very interesting, dear, but I can't really believe you. Can you blame me?

Not a Time for Anger

Imagine that your best friend laughs at you when you tell her about your psychic experiences. Of *course* you want to pound your fists on the wall, run out of the room, or cry. You are having one of the most important experiences in your life—you may even feel you are going through a spiritual transformation—and a person you love is *not* taking you seriously. This is devastating! You feel abandoned and separated from your loved one. Her negative statements create a deep emotional crisis in you. *Even so, stop, take a deep breath, and do not react too quickly.* Right now, you need to understand that your friend is confused and possibly frightened by the psychic experiences you are sharing. Hang in there, because if you get angry, you may dig yourself into a deep hole.

Cool Your Hurt and Angry Feelings

Before you lash out in anger or start to cry, consider the following questions.

- Why should your loved one believe you if he or she has never had the experiences you've had? Would you? Maybe not.

- Do you agree with all of your loved one's opinions about other people, the world, politics, religion, and so on? Do you have all the same friends and like all the same people? Why expect your loved one to believe and agree with everything you say?

- Do you need your loved one's approval so badly that you cannot have an interest that your loved one does not share with you?

If you are able to refrain from trying to cram your beliefs down your loved one's throat, you will have an opportunity to gain his or her support. Notice the word is "support," not "agreement" or "approval." No one wants to be told they *have* to believe in something, particularly when it comes to psychic and mediumistic experiences. When you talk about your experiences, you may unknowingly push an emotional button in your loved one's subconscious, and he or she may become scared to death. *Psychic stories put many people into fear mode.* We live in a skeptical world that has brainwashed most of us into thinking that people who are psychic are "seeing things." Well yes, we *are* seeing things, but those of us who are educated about what we are "seeing" understand that we are not making this all up, thank you very much! If your loved one has bought into this brainwash about psychic experience, it is unlikely that he or she can compute what you are saying.

Sample Dialogues of What to Say to Skeptical Loved Ones

"It is hard to know what is happening with me. I am seeing things that others don't see and it is quite possible that I have some psychic abilities. I need to learn more about psychic experiences. I don't ask you to believe me; just support me in my curiosity to learn more about what I am experiencing."

"I understand that you feel I am making up stories when I make comments about what others are thinking. And it is possible that you are correct. But it is also possible that I am tuning in on the thoughts of another person. Maybe I am psychic. I need to learn more about psychic experiences. Can you keep an open mind and support me as I explore this?"

"Since I have known you, you have been skeptical about anything 'psychic.' I understand why listening to me talk about psychic experiences is hard for you. I respect your skepticism and quite frankly, I would be as skeptical as you are if I were not having these experiences. I do not ask you to believe my experiences. I ask you to understand that I am having them, and they feel quite unusual. Please be supportive as I learn about these experiences."

Use one of the above responses when you are attacked emotionally. It would be all too easy to scream "Shut up, you don't know what you're talking about" or some other unpleasant phrase not appropriate for print. If you do not like my suggested responses, create your own diplomatic responses.

Take the Pressure OFF

If you are in a love relationship, take the pressure off your partner. Once your partner understands that you do not expect him or her to believe in everything you experience, life will get better. Next you can ask your partner, "Does it bother you if I talk about my experiences as they happen on a day-to-day basis?" If your partner says something like "To be honest, sweetheart, when you tell me these stories about seeing dead people, it creeps me out," then you know that you have to take things *very* slowly, and not report all of your experiences as they happen. You are much better off joining a spiritual circle where you can make new friends and share your experiences.

Make sure your partner is not jealous of your new friends. Make it clear that you need to meet others who have an interest in understanding psychic and mediumistic phenomena. You have a particular interest in spiritual experiences and need people with whom to share this interest, just as people who like baseball enjoy talking about what happened last night at the ball game with other sports fans. Let your partner know that anytime he or she wants to hear more about your experiences, you are happy to talk, but that you do not want to compromise the relationship by talking *too* much.

You may feel a bit sad if you have a partner who is a skeptic. Before you started having these experiences, you could talk to your partner about *everything,* and now you can't. If you are in a strong relationship, it can survive and even be enriched by the fact that the two of you are both growing. You can grow and become unique individuals together.

Be Tolerant

I admit it: I would never want to be married to another psychic medium. I am absolutely thrilled to be married to a guy who watches football, plays pool on the computer, and who, while incredibly supportive of my work, does not totally buy into it. He is not nearly as sensitive to anything as I am, and quite frankly I do not know how he stands living with me sometimes. I am *so* sensitive to sound; I complain if he plays any music that I do not like. He can tolerate it when I play music *he* doesn't like, but I literally cannot stand it when his music is on. I am picky, picky, picky! Do I sound like a fun person to live with?

I'm also extremely sensitive to scents that my partner cannot even smell. And people? I can't go out and socialize with folks I do not feel comfortable with. My sensitivity is a real "pain in the you-know-what" for people who are close to me! And excuse me for saying so, but you may not be easy to live with either. Give those non-psychics around you a break. Be tolerant of their disbelief. Keep in mind that they have to put up with a lot as they cope with your special sensitivities.

Some of My Best Friends Are Non-Psychics

Have as many non-psychic friends as possible. While it is sometimes lonely for those of us who are psychic and mediumistic, we need balance in our lives. When we do not mix with non-psychics, we can become obsessed with our internal experiences. This is not emotionally healthy. While it is wonderful that we are able to have psychic and mediumistic experiences, we also need to keep our physical feet planted on earth.

I need to be around people who transmit a kind of "energy" that my psychic friends do not usually transmit. For me, non-psychics create a different vibrational environment than my terribly sensitive psychic friends create. These often sports-minded non-psychics yell and scream, have another beer, and laugh a lot. These sports buddies eat hot dogs instead of sprouts. I find this refreshing after spending time with my psychic group, who incessantly talk about the newest weird spirit guides that have come into their lives. I hope you will look for balance as you discover your psychic talents. Don't kick "civilians" out of your life.

You do *not* have to tell all your non-psychic friends that you *are* psychic. Can you imagine my going up to some non-psychic guy and saying, "I love being around you because you create a different vibrational environment for me"? Before he ran the other way, he would most likely throw his beer at me in order to protect himself.

Non-Psychics Are Often Bigtime Intuitives

Perhaps it is naughty of me to use the term "non-psychic," because some of the non-psychic people who seem so dense can be *very intuitive.* These people have gut feelings and hunches that pay off bigtime! They may not see spirits, but they do things like make a million dollars because they "just know" when to sell a business. Their great insights and intuitions allow them to be incredibly successful.

My two best girlfriends are non-psychics. They are extremely sensitive individuals; otherwise, I am sure they could not put up with me. Both are interested in their children and in music, and we talk about those topics the most. Yes, of course, I share stories with them about my work, but not in the way I do with my best psychic friend, a guy who works with me. He and I talk mostly about our psychic experiences and development. I also enjoy relationships with my core students, as we have the same interests. I have several other psychic friends, but I prefer to have as many non-psychic friends as possible. I do not want to always be thinking about what visions I have had, or what happened in the last reading I gave.

I do not give my non-psychic friends readings, even if they ask me. I do not peer into their minds when I am with them. My friendships are healthier when I do not try to be someone's close friend and psychic at the same time. Plus, I know too much about my friends, and it would be hard for me to give a close friend a professional reading—after all, the whole point of the reading is for me to see things *of which I have no knowledge.*

I have learned how to turn my psychic and mediumistic switch to the "off" position. I was fortunate to take courses with some great organizations: the Arthur Findlay College of Great Britain, the American Federation of Spiritualist Churches, and the Morris Pratt Institute in the United States. I studied very hard, taking both written courses and classroom work with great teachers. I wanted to learn to manage my gifts and have a somewhat normal life. I say "somewhat normal" because my life has never been the same since I discovered my gifts. By this time, most of my loved ones know that I am a psychic medium, and some I talk to more openly than others. I have calmed down, but my life as a psychic was not always as settled as it is now.

Carole Lynne's Story

In my "mature years," I feel I am a fairly well-adjusted psychic medium. With years of study and professional experience behind me, I am finally coming into my own and can honestly say I am a happy psychic! Of course there are always difficulties managing all of the emotions that come along with being extra sensitive. As I look back, I realize that becoming a happy psychic has been a challenging journey.

The Early Years of My Marriage: Not so Easy!

I wish I had known how to talk about my experiences in the early years of my marriage! There we were, my husband and I, attending parties in New York City's Greenwich Village. At one party I turned to my husband and said, "Did you speak to that divorced woman standing over there wearing the red dress?" He responded, "How do you know she is divorced? She did not say anything about being divorced." I responded, "She looks divorced. Don't you see that?" And he responded "*No,* and I wish you would stop making up stories about people when you have absolutely no evidence that what you are saying is true. You have a very vivid imagination."

I cannot remember how many times he and I had conversations like that. For years I felt my greater self shrink back into my body so that I would not "see" things about people. Maybe I *was* making it up? Was my husband right about my imagination, or was I really seeing things *he could not see?* It was confusing because I would often learn that what I had seen was absolutely true. And if he was not seeing the same things I was seeing, how could I blame him for thinking I was making things up? It was as if my eyes were able to see a red balloon that his eyes could not see. Why should he believe that I saw a red balloon that for him *simply was not there?*

I was confused about my psychic nature for many years. However, I was busy being a musician and raising two children, so understanding my psychic nature was not a priority. I pushed that part of me into a dark corner; to be honest, I was not interested or ready to know myself completely at that time. Later in life I was bopped on the head by so many spiritual experiences that it became impossible for me to avoid myself any longer. I was in my forties when I began the process of accepting my psychic and mediumistic gifts.

Living in a Mostly Non-Psychic Family

I was fortunate to marry a person who was interested in psychic experiences even though he did not have them himself. I was also fortunate that my mediumistic experiences began when my children were grown up. As I said before, going from psychic experiences to mediumistic experiences is a huge jump. My family could accept that I was intuitive and psychic, but I do not know how I would have explained to my small children that I was seeing the spirits of people who had died. On the other hand, if I had been seeing spirits when they were little, I am sure I would have found a way to educate them. I do notice that now I do not share a lot about my spiritual experiences with my grandchildren. Their parents do not all believe in what I do for work, and I simply would rather not get into a family hassle. Plus, it is nice to forget about seeing spirits and play with my grandkids like other grandmothers do.

I am sure some psychics and mediums will think I am putting myself down by not entirely coming out of the psychic closet with my family. Of course *they* know I am a professional psychic medium and author, but I am selective about which family members I talk to *openly* about my work. With some family members I am expansive—I share on a deep level. These people regularly ask me questions about my readings, what I am writing, and how I feel when I see spirits. While they may or may not believe in what I experience, I feel their genuine interest in my work.

There are others in my family who do not seem comfortable when I talk about my work. While they are polite and listen to me, they do not respond with questions. I feel like they don't hear me when I talk to them. I notice that they change the topic of conversation rather quickly. At times this frustrates me and hurts my feelings. But I suspect that those who do not show an interest are probably very skeptical about my visions, and they know that if they talk openly with me about their skepticism, they may hurt me. I can understand where they may be coming from. Though I am sad to be hiding part of myself from my loved ones, it is not important for me to stand on a soapbox and try to convince them. They have a right to their skeptic mindsets just as much as I have a right to see things the way I do.

I feel very good about myself and my spiritual gifts. But I also know that what I do and believe in is unusual, and I do not want to try to influence anyone to believe as I do.

Even when I suspect a loved one has psychic qualities, I do not try to enlist them. If a family member is meant to have these experiences, the spirits will tap him on the shoulder and let him know of their existence, just as they did for me. It is not my responsibility to inform others about their gifts.

Some Unfortunate Breakups

While you do not have to abandon the skeptics in your life, some relationships may deteriorate as you discover your psychic self. For instance, when I was in the process of realizing I was a medium, I met another woman who was married and had two school-age children. She was also starting to understand that she was a medium. We studied in some of the same seminars. She was not as fortunate as I was to have a supportive husband. As time went on, their relationship changed and their marriage eventually ended.

In the worst-case scenarios, relationships end, parents tell their psychic children to stop imagining things, and psychic people are diagnosed with mental illness because their visions have been misunderstood as hallucinations. In my experience, genuine psychic and mediumistic experience has always had a sacred quality. There are no negative energies; I can receive messages when I choose to and turn off that part of myself when I choose to. In addition, when I am giving a reading and bring evidence to a client about someone in spirit—information I have no prior knowledge of—then it is clear that I am truly communicating with spirit.

Caution: People with mental problems and neurological disorders may have hallucinations that need medical treatment. Telling the difference between mental challenges and psychic experiences can be very difficult. People who are receiving negative messages and who say they are "possessed" and have no control over what is happening to them should see a mental health professional immediately.

Talking to Acquaintances, Strangers, and Coworkers

One of the biggest mistakes people make when they begin to have psychic experiences is to tell *everyone* they know. You must find some people to confide in because it could become emotionally unhealthy for you to go through such huge changes by yourself. And of course you are going to confide in your loved ones and closest friends. But what about confiding in strangers, acquaintances, and coworkers? *Be selective!*

Strangers

Do you want to talk to the stranger next to you on the plane about your psychic experiences? Sure, go ahead if you like. You will never see this person again, and if she is not interested, she will either go to sleep or start watching a movie (which may be a real good deal for you if you want to sleep).

Coworkers

For the most part, I suggest you *not* talk about psychic and mediumistic experiences at work unless you work for a yoga center, New Age magazine, or other "spirit-friendly" business. You might get into a difficult situation—for example, say your coworker's religion denounces those who have visions, and that person complains about you to the boss. There may be people in your workplace who are terrified of so-called "evil spirits" and if anything goes wrong at work, *you* may be accused of bringing bad spirits to work *with* you. While your boss might never admit that it was the stories about you and the evil spirits that got you fired, management might find another reason to either downgrade your position or remove you from staff entirely.

Then there are those coworkers who believe in curses (I don't). They may be suspicious of you. Unfortunately, people have all kinds of strange ideas and fears about spirit communication, and if someone gets "spooked" by your psychic and mediumistic experiences, the whole situation may take on a life of its own and you will wish you had *never* been open about your experiences at work.

The other night I was having dinner with some friends who are part of the psychic community. When I said that I advised most of my students to not talk about their psychic experiences at work, one woman's eyes widened and she looked at me as if I had suggested that we all stop fighting for human rights issues. I added, "Well, what would it be like if a schoolteacher started talking about her psychic and mediumistic experiences in her classroom? Not all of the parents would appreciate that." My friend's expression changed immediately and she was more understanding of my comment.

Even though some of you have talked about your psychic experiences at work with no negative results, I still give the warning that this is not a good idea in many workplaces.

Close Friends

Before talking to a friend, remind yourself to be respectful of the fact that hearing stories of your psychic experiences may be difficult for a skeptical friend. You will not really know until you begin to speak. Following are some suggested dialogues to use when speaking to a friend about your experiences for the first time.

"I know that what I am going to tell you may sound a bit strange, but as we are so close I want you to know what I am experiencing. I am having some extremely vivid dreams, and in these dreams I am learning about things that happen in my waking life. For instance, I had a dream the other night that there would be an accident at the bottom of our road, and the next day there was an accident. Perhaps it was a coincidence, but I have had quite a few dreams now about things that are going to happen, and those things do happen. Naturally I am very curious about what is going on with me, so I am attending a seminar on dreams next week."

"I need to tell you about some experiences I am having. Lately I feel as if there are spirits around me. I want to make it clear that these spirits do not feel dangerous and I am not afraid. I feel wonderful when I have these experiences. What I feel is a presence of something that is not like anything I have ever felt before. The other day at a friend's house, when I was feeling the presence of a spirit, I had a vision of a man standing by my friend's front door, and I felt the man was telling me he was the spirit of a man whose name was Bob. When I shared this with my friend, she said she had an uncle named Bob and I had described him perfectly. Since that day, I have had a number of similar experiences. To be honest, I have never believed those who have said they have seen spirits, but now that I have had these experiences, I am curious about what is happening. I do not feel that I am imagining all this. So I have contacted a mediumship teacher and I am going to sit in a spiritual circle to try to understand what is going on with me. I do not expect you to believe in this. What I do ask is that you be supportive of me as I explore these experiences."

These dialogues are only samples of what you might say. Obviously, your statements have to reflect your experiences. As you share your experiences with others, there are two things you want to make sure you stress:

1. I do not expect you to believe in my experiences.

2. I do not feel anything negative around me.

Do not make the person you are confiding in feel pressured in any way to believe in what you are experiencing or to become interested in exploring spirit communication. This is *your* interest. *You also want to avoid scaring them.* Many people will automatically assume that spirits must be evil. This unfortunate reaction may come as a result of watching too many scary movies or visiting so-called haunted houses. Some religious people are taught that they should beware when spirits come around.

Be calm and brave as you talk to your family and friends, and do not feel compelled to talk to everyone. Again, be selective and take your time as you relate to others about your spiritual experiences.

Some Psychic Topics Are Safer Than Others

You may not make anyone's hair stand on end when you talk about simple experiences like knowing who is calling when the phone rings. Many people have enough intuition to have experiences like that. But if you have a psychic premonition that someone is going to die that comes true, many will have a hard time believing this experience unless they have had a similar experience. And if you start having mediumistic experiences where you have visions of those who have passed on and receive messages from these spirits, you are crossing a line that many people simply cannot cross without becoming fearful.

Intuitive and psychic experiences are understood more easily by the "general public" than mediumistic experiences, which are often understood *only* by those who have had their own mediumistic experiences or received a great reading from a medium who has brought them undeniable evidence that the spirit is indeed communicating through the medium.

When People Are in Grief

I find it interesting to observe how normally skeptical people react *differently* when the death of someone close to them occurs. A death will sometimes create an environment in which the family and friends of the deceased will come to believe in visions of those who have passed on. For instance, people who are grieving may have spiritual visions of the recently departed person. Because they are going through an emotional time, these people might tell family members and friends about their visions. The others are more likely to believe those who have had visions because the whole group is in deep grief. But I have heard of many cases where several years later, those who *believed* the visions have *changed their minds* about them as the years have gone by. They have decided that they all had visions because they were grieving.

Many people who are *not* psychic or mediumistic *do* have visions of their loved ones shortly after a death has occurred. For many this is a one-time experience. I firmly believe that almost anyone can have a spiritual vision of his or her own loved one after that loved one has passed on. This will *not* be a one-time experience for those who are truly psychic and mediumistic—they will not only have visions of their *own* loved ones, but visions of others who have passed on who are *not* related to them and who they have never even known.

Special Challenges for Psychic People

Meeting new people can be challenging. While I wish it were not so, I have found that since I have been brave enough to be open as a Spiritualist minister, psychic medium, and author, people treat me differently than they did when I was working as a musician in clubs and a presentation skills coach in the business world. People were enthusiastic about talking to a musician and asked me what kind of guitar strings to buy and how long it took to learn to play guitar. Business people talked to me about their stage fright before giving presentations. Now, if someone (who is not part of our psychic community) asks "what do you do?" and I say that I am a psychic medium and author, you could hear a pin drop. Some people stiffen up a bit and then ask, "Can you see any spirits around me now?" or "Are you picking up anything about my life right now?" I reply that like other professionals, I have "office hours" and I turn off the switch within that allows me to see spirits and know things about people to protect the privacy of others.

Another special challenge is learning to discern which people within our psychic community can become trusted friends. One cannot assume that just because someone says they are doing spiritual work, they are automatically sincere and honest.

We Who "See" Must Become Strong and Tolerant

If you want to be liked and approved of by everyone (and most of us do,) then you will have to work hard to become stronger and more independent. Have a serious talk with your ego and tell it that you are not going to get rave reviews from everyone you meet. Tell your ego in no uncertain terms that "those days are over, kid." Those of us who have psychic and mediumistic experiences have to become *very strong* people, because many people in our lives will not understand or approve of our deep interest in psychic sensitivity.

While it is uncomfortable for me to be around people who do not approve of me, I have to remind myself that I do not always accept the beliefs of everyone I meet. I have to remember how grateful I am to live in a country where differences are more accepted than in some other parts of the world. In our country we have the freedom to practice Spiritualism, which supports a belief in spirit communication. Psychics and mediums also freely open New Age stores and spiritual centers where many kinds of readings are given. We are free to write books and articles, and place advertisements about our work. The subject of "what happens after death" is a very personal and controversial subject. Personal freedom allows people to have their own beliefs. If we truly believe in personal freedom, then we have to respect the fact that many do not believe as we do.

It is not always easy for us to live in a skeptical world. I have had conversations with colleagues who also work as psychic mediums. Some of us express feelings of loneliness. Many of us are the only psychics in our families. We long for more people who can truly understand us.

All "Spiritual" People Are Not Created Equal

When I first joined a spiritual circle, I was *so* excited to be with people who were like me that I made an *assumption* that because these people were in spiritual groups, I could trust them more than people who were not psychic and mediumistic. While some of my new friends were wonderful and still close friends today, I made some huge mistakes as I became involved in new friendships. I became blinded to the fact that this person was a liar or that person was a gossip. *All I cared about was finding people to believe and understand me.* I was vulnerable and naïve—uncomfortable in our skeptical world and looking for validation from anyone like me. Now I understand that *all* groups, from bowling leagues to charity organizations, are made up of some wonderful people and some people I would not care to be friends with.

Do not kid yourself into believing that just because an individual claims to be spiritual or is a member of a so-called spiritual group, he or she can be trusted. Be selective when you choose friends, no matter where you are!

You Can Learn to Survive in a Skeptical World

I am very happy as a psychic medium because I have learned to be *selective* as I decide who to talk to and what to say. I do not need everyone's approval. Having taken the pressure off my loved ones and friends to believe in what I believe in, I now have wonderful relationships, with people whether they believe me or not. I have also found some new psychic and mediumistic friends. The world is filled with wonderful people and we do not have to share similar ideas. How boring would that be?

Following is a list of important points to review as you learn to communicate with your loved ones, friends, coworkers, and strangers.

1. It is not important for every person in your life to know about the psychic experiences you have. Be selective, particularly at work.

2. It is not important that everyone approves of your psychic experiences.

3. You do not have to leave your family, friends, or lovers because you are "different." You can work with those you love and gain their support.

4. You do have to carefully select some new friends who are also psychic, to add balance to your life.

FOUR

Finding the Helpers You Need

You know the TV warnings that say "don't try this at home"? It is with great sincerity that I send a personal warning from me to you: *do not walk the spiritual path alone.* In this chapter you will learn how to find teachers, spiritual groups, friends, and if need be, "spirit-friendly" therapists.

Trust me—the spiritual path is not a walk to take by yourself, especially if you are having psychic and mediumistic experiences! If you want to make a decision about how your gifts fit into your life, you need direction from a professional. I could have saved myself years of upset and anxiety had I known how to find people who could help me with my gifts. I was so clueless that I did not even know the word "medium" until someone told me *that* was what I was.

Those of us who are blessed with psychic and mediumistic spiritual gifts need to learn to understand these gifts under the guidance of a spiritual teacher or within a religion such as Spiritualism, which honors the practice of spirit communication. A teacher can help you decide if you simply want to *understand* your gifts or if you also want to *expand* your gifts. They can help you find a way to share your gifts with others in volunteer or professional work.

As you explore and develop your spiritual talents, beware of groups and individuals that sensationalize your unique gifts. People who do not develop spiritually as they receive psychic and mediumistic gifts often get into psychological trouble or become addicted to the flashy side of spirit communication. These are the people who want to visit haunted houses for the wrong reasons and who are drawn to negative energies. Again, this is my personal bias, and while I do not mean to step on the toes of some of my colleagues who are drawn to such things, I encourage my students to stay away from things that aggrandize spirit communication. I want them to focus on spiritual development and to always remember that communication with spirit is a sacred practice.

Along the same lines, be discerning about so-called "ghostbusting" groups that visit houses said to have spirit activity. I respect the groups that are not into sensationalism. Instead, they use scientific methods to try to prove or disprove that spirit activity exists in a particular location. I also respect those mediums who feel truly devoted to helping spirits that seem to be stuck in so-called haunted places. These mediums feel drawn to this kind of work out of compassion for the spirits. They are not the typical spirit groupies who run from one haunted house to the next because it is so exciting and spooky. My advice to you is that if you need some "spookiness," save it for Halloween and create the greatest ghost costume ever!

What If You Don't Want to Develop Your Gifts?

If you are sure that you do not want to develop your psychic and mediumistic gifts, then let these experiences be part of your life without paying much attention to them. Allow experiences to happen and don't make a big deal out of them. If you get overexcited and call all your friends to talk about the incredible vision you had, you will only encourage these experiences to continue. Pray to the God of your understanding that you only want psychic and mediumistic experiences of the highest spiritual quality—those that can enhance your life.

The Importance of Education

Some of you may feel that you are being called, by the God of your understanding, to develop your gifts in order to help others.

If you have questions about whether your experiences are authentic, you will find out when they are *validated* at a spiritual class or circle. I like circles that are facilitated by Spiritualist ministers, professional psychics, or psychic mediums. In a circle, you will do readings for other students (sitters) under the direction of your teacher. Some of the readings will be called psychic or intuitive: you will be communicating with *the spirit of the living person* you are doing the reading for. You will understand many things about the nature of your sitter, including his or her best qualities and life challenges, and hopefully you will bring him or her helpful guidance from the world of spirit. In this kind of reading you will *not* be receiving the guidance from your sitter's loved ones in spirit, but from the spiritual guides whom I prefer to call "Guidance."

Your teacher may offer both psychic and mediumistic exercises. In a Spiritualist circle, mediumistic exercises will be included; spirit communication is one of the sacred practices of Spiritualism. In these readings you communicate with *the spirit of one who has passed on* and who has a message for your sitter. We call this "linking with the communicating spirit." You will describe your visions of those who have passed on, in the hopes that your sitter will recognize the spirit you are describing. This will be a very important experience for you, because if your sitter can recognize the person you are describing—a person who has lived a life on this earth *whom you know nothing about*—then you will have *proof* that you really are connecting with spirits. We call this "proving survival." Read more about this in my books *How to Get a Good Reading from a Psychic Medium* and *Cosmic Connection: Messages for a Better World.*

High Standards

Select a teacher with high standards who demands that the evidence you bring is complete enough to prove that a true communication with spirit is taking place. Poor evidence would sound like this: "I feel I have the spirit of your grandmother here. She was old when she passed and had straight gray hair that was thinning quite a bit." This is not enough evidence; many people have grandmothers who would fit that description. Good evidence would sound like this: "I feel I have the spirit of your grandmother here. She was old when she passed and had straight gray hair that was thinning quite a bit. As I feel closer to her spirit, I feel that she died of lung problems, most likely cancer. She lets me know that she has three sisters, two of which are in spirit with her and one who is still living. I hear that the names Kate, Robert, and Sylvia are in the family."

As you can see, the second example is more detailed and specific. The person you are reading for may not understand all of the evidence you bring, but your goal is to link closely enough with a spirit that most of the evidence is understood. Have patience. Some very talented psychic mediums sat in class for years before they were able to link with spirits consistently.

Teachers Help You Create Boundaries

One of the most important reasons to join a spiritual circle is to have the help of a teacher as you learn to set boundaries with the world of spirit. Good teachers tell students not to do unrequested readings. Learning to set boundaries is *the* most important aspect of psychic and mediumistic education. Let us briefly explore the topic of boundaries in order to give you an idea of what you will be learning from an experienced teacher.

As many of us are first opening up to the world of spirit, we will feel the presence of the spirits of people who have passed on—this may happen anytime, anywhere! These spirits, once they have our attention, will try to give us messages to pass on to their loved ones who are still living. It is necessary that those of us who have not yet realized we are mediums *have* these initial experiences. Without these experiences, we might never discover our spiritual gifts.

However necessary these *initial* contacts from spirit may be, they can be troublesome until we have set boundaries. For instance, you may suddenly feel the presence of a spirit close to a total stranger who is walking down the street. Or you may feel the presence of a spirit near a friend while having dinner in a restaurant. Because the presence of spirits is so new to you, you may feel compelled to go up to a stranger on the street and tell her about the spirit near her. You may feel compelled to tell your friend in a restaurant that a spirit has a message for her. However, it is not a good idea to give readings to anyone who has not requested a reading, especially a stranger! While I realize it is tempting to go up to a woman in the supermarket when you suddenly sense that the spirit of her daughter, who passed on last year, is near her, I recommend that you do not act on this impulse. What right do you have to approach a complete stranger and tell her the spirit of her daughter is next to her? What if she is part of a religion that frowns on spirit communication? She may be horrified. And she may wonder *who you think you are* to assume that you are communicating with a loved one of *hers.* What if she is in such a state of grief that hearing your news throws her into a state of shock right there in the market?

In my opinion, you and I have no more right to go up to a stranger with a message from spirit than a doctor has to approach a stranger and announce "I suspect you are suffering from undiagnosed diabetes." No professional and ethical doctor would ever do anything like that, and in my opinion no professional and ethical psychic medium would either.

While we know that some television mediums are going up to strangers while they are being filmed, keep in mind that this creates a good television show. I and many of my colleagues shudder when we see mediums on television working in this manner. In fairness to the producers of such shows, I realize that they may have received permission from the people the mediums approach. However, as my students and clients watch these shows, they get the impression that it is okay for a medium to go up to a total stranger and give an unrequested reading. Other television mediums do demonstrations of spirit communication for an audience. This situation is entirely different and totally ethical, as the audience has made a choice to attend the demonstration.

I am so strongly against bringing messages to people who are not expecting to hear them that when I was invited to be the Spiritualist speaker at a church of another religion, I refused to do a demonstration of spirit communication during the traditional church service. I told the minister who invited me that because spirit communication was not a tradition in their religion and those attending the service would not be expecting messages from those who had passed on, I would prefer that the church offer a demonstration of spirit communication later that day. People would then be able to elect to attend the demonstration and would be expecting to see me work as a medium. The minister agreed, and both the service and the demonstration later that day were well received.

Students ask me if they can give messages to their best friends. If you are with your best friend whom you know is open to spirit communication, then you might make an exception to this rule and give her the message. I admit that as a new medium, I made a few exceptions and gave a couple friends messages from spirit when I was not involved in a professional appointment or class situation. But in both cases, the people involved were *close* friends of mine and I asked their permission before telling them about the spirits I was seeing around them. These days, as an experienced medium, I almost never give anyone a message outside a formal reading. I know that I do my best work when I am in a scheduled session and have adequately prepared.

Although it is understandable that as a new psychic and/or medium you feel *compelled* to deliver an unrequested message, how are you to overcome this need? First, set boundaries. Tell the world of spirit that you are not available 24/7! This boundary can be set with a simple prayer to the God of your understanding. "Dear God, I pray that those in spirit who wish to communicate through me with messages for their loved ones only do so when I have sent out a prayer asking for those in spirit to communicate."

Second, if you are not already part of a spiritual class or circle, join one! In a class, you will have a designated time and place to communicate with spirit, and you may not feel as compelled to do readings outside of class. Your teacher will instruct you on how to open up to spirit and how to close down as you are concluding your period of communication. Stop doing what are often called "Readings on the Run"—unsolicited readings. If you do not become part of a spiritual circle in order to receive the education you need, you will likely have spirits trying to contact you at any hour of the day. The best mediums set boundaries and demand that spirits communicate only *when invited to do so*. Your spiritual development and your quality of life will be much greater if you set strict boundaries.

Remember that working with spirit is sacred. Readings should take place in a sacred environment, not on a street corner or at a bar.

Finding a Teacher

I prefer the teachers connected to Spiritualist organizations rather than those who are unaffiliated, unless their background began in Spiritualism. Many well-known mediums today, while no longer as connected to the religion of Spiritualism due to their intense professional schedules, studied within this religion for many years. Why Spiritualism? Because this religion believes in God, the afterlife, *and* that those who have received the gift of mediumistic talent can communicate with those in the afterlife. I was brought up in another religion that did not accept my communications with the world of spirit. I found becoming a Spiritualist was like coming home to myself. However, many other mediums I know have not left their original religion, but have simply taken classes within Spiritualist churches or at spiritual centers.

In the resource section of this book you will find the names of Spiritualist organizations.

Some of you may not wish to be associated with a religion. You may also find good teachers in the directories of New Age magazines or in New Age bookstores. In these cases, find out about the educational background and professional experience of the teacher you are considering. Do not be afraid to ask a prospective teacher about his or her background.

Consistent Study

When a psychic or medium starts giving readings before he or she is ready, it is a shame for both the reader and their client. Many students rush to start work as readers and do not take the needed time to develop their gifts. No teacher can make a person who has not been blessed with these gifts into a psychic or a medium, but a good teacher can train a student in the ethics involved. He or she can also teach students how to get the best evidence in order to prove that an actual spirit communication is going on. For a fuller explanation of "evidence," please read my book *How to Get a Good Reading from a Psychic Medium.*

A good teacher will ask you to commit to a number of sessions and insist on consistent participation in classes. He or she will train you to be an expert or not want to train you at all. Why would a good teacher want to feel responsible for putting psychics and mediums who are not adequately trained out into the world as professionals?

I ask students to choose one main teacher and then supplement their education with seminars given by other teachers. I do not coax anyone to choose me as his or her main teacher, but if they do, I have rather strict requirements about consistent study over a period of time. While I applaud teachers with strict rules about consistent study, I am not happy with teachers who coach people using harsh words. I have seen students come out of psychic and mediumistic classes crying their eyes out. Many talented people have been crushed by ego-driven teachers.

Fortunately, I avoided studying with any harsh teachers and had a wonderful experience during the ten years I devoted to developing my mediumship. I will be grateful to my teachers for the rest of my life and into eternity. My two best teachers both told me that they were *not* my teachers and that Spirit was my *real* teacher. They were there to facilitate my becoming closer to Spirit (or the God of your understanding). I now tell my own students the same thing, and I believe it. I am not their teacher. I create the environment and organize classes where I can encourage them to become close to Spirit.

Patience Is Necessary

Once you find the right teacher and commit yourself to years of study and practice, pray for patience. As I look back on my early psychic and mediumistic class experiences, I see that sometimes my information was correct, and sometimes it was not. It took years for me to be able to bring consistent correct information in both psychic and mediumistic readings. I needed to develop the necessary "psychic stamina." My teacher had me build up to it slowly, adding more readings and demonstrations every few months. Many new students think that because they are able to do a few good readings, they are ready for professional work.

However, we have to build up the stamina in the same way that athletes have to train over many years.

Cautions

I stay away from teachers and groups that believe they can change behavior or remove curses. Some of my clients have shared with me that they have paid psychics thousands of dollars to remove a so-called curse or bring their boyfriend back to them. I admit that there may be paranormal experiences that I do not understand, but for me, these practices are not real and I do not feel comfortable being associated with any teacher or group that talks about curses.

Beware of individuals who want to be everyone's guru. I protected myself and did not study with anyone who would try to brainwash me into a certain kind of spiritual thinking. I have always felt comfortable with teachers who express their strong opinions, but who encourage me to come to my own conclusions. I listened to what other students said about various teachers, and if a teacher sounded too egocentric, I stayed away. Unfortunately, some teachers who are incredibly gifted as psychics and mediums are not able to handle the power they have been given, and their egos swell up. They feel extremely superior to others and are quite hard on their students.

Opinions and Politics

As you study, be prepared for many differences of opinion about what true mediumship is. Our community, like any community, is made up of many different people with various ideas. Some people get so frustrated with the differences of opinion and politics that seem to be part of any organized group that they stop studying too early. Study as long as you need to—many study for ten years or more. Let the differences and the politics roll off your back as you remember that your *higher purpose* is to be grateful for your spiritual gifts and to develop them in a sacred manner.

When Psychics and Mediums Work Professionally

If you ultimately decide to give up your job so that you can be a psychic or medium, be prepared for criticism. Many professional mediums are accused of being unspiritual and egotistical because they charge a fee. In most cases these mediums have given up other jobs with benefits to start their own practices, and have *all* of the expenses that self-employed people have, *without* any of the benefits of a company job. And the more famous the psychic medium, the higher the expenses—famous people need large staffs to deal with thousands of inquiries and prepare for national and international tours. Some even need security guards. One medium said, "When the spirit world finds a way to pay all my bills, then I will do readings for free. But until then, I need to charge a fee like any other professional."

If you need a low-cost reading, there are many readers who volunteer at Spiritualist church fundraising days. Readings are often twenty dollars and the donations collected support the church.

I do not judge psychics and mediums by their decision to be volunteers or professionals. I do not assume that very famous readers have "sold out" to big business. What I look for is a psychic or medium who is spiritually evolved. I feel good in the presence of such a person. I know they care deeply about the service they are providing. Just as there are good and not-so-good doctors, lawyers, plumbers, and carpenters, there are good and not-so-good psychics and mediums. Our field is no different than any other professional field.

I recommend that you read my books *Cosmic Connection: Messages for a Better World* and *How to Get a Good Reading from a Psychic Medium.* You will gain a deep understanding of the experiences I have had as a psychic medium and inspirational channel.

Finding the Right Therapist

The title of this book is *Are You Psychic or Making It Up?* for good reason. Most of us who start having psychic, mediumistic, or so-called "paranormal experiences" begin to question our sanity.

Experiences with the world of spirit have been very positive and uplifting. I have found this to be true in the classes I attended as a student, in classes I have taught, and when I have given individual and group readings. Negative thoughts are not part of the spiritual experience when we communicate with the world of spirit. Negativity should not be part of the experience. Should you experience negativity, please be aware of the following warning.

Warning: If your experiences with spirit feel negative to you, then seek medical help from a therapist or minister who has an appreciation for spiritual experience and spirit communication. If you feel your house is occupied by spirits, consult with a group that visits locations to identify spirit activity (often called "ghostbusters"). *If, on the other hand, you or anyone you know has suicidal thoughts, get immediate help from a suicide hotline or emergency room. These kinds of negative thoughts have nothing to do with spirit communication.*

Psychics Can Be Extra Sensitive

As you open up to the world of spirit, you may become more sensitive than the average person, and your feelings may be easily hurt. Being extra-sensitive can be difficult. Many sensitive people benefit from therapy as they learn how to handle their wide range of emotions. Therapy is an incredible tool for personal growth, and you do not have to have a mental illness diagnosis in order to benefit. If you choose to look for a therapist, please find a "spirit-friendly" therapist.

Why "Spirit-Friendly"?

A therapist who is totally closed-minded to all psychic and mediumistic phenomena (often called "paranormal phenomena" by the mainstream world) may insist that what *you* feel may be spiritual or psychic/mediumistic experiences are in fact hallucinations. In my experience, unless a student has a mental challenge that demands psychiatric help, most students have some spiritual experiences that are authentic and some that are imagined. As said before, it is normal for students doing psychic and mediumistic exercises to struggle as they learn to sense the difference between authentic messages from spirit and thoughts from their own mind. As a teacher of mediumship, I do not see this as a symptom of mental problems.

I am concerned about psychic and mediumistic people who are under the care of a closed-minded therapist. This does not mean that I think a therapist should accept all psychic and mediumistic experiences as reported by patients to be authentic. But I would hope a student of spiritual experience would find a therapist open to the idea that some of what the student was experiencing could be authentic, and that he or she would not immediately dismiss all spiritual visions as hallucinations. It goes without saying that if a student is having negative experiences and feels possessed by spirits, there is most likely a psychological problem that demands treatment.

If you decide to see a therapist, you will become well acquainted with your personal issues, and that will help you to discern when you might be adding some of your own thoughts to an otherwise authentic spirit communication.

Finding a Spirit-Friendly Therapist

"Spirit-friendly" therapists are out there. The more I talk to therapist friends of mine, the more I realize how many therapists have had spiritual experiences, but would never tell anyone in their professional life. They are "in the closet" about their so-called paranormal experiences. I understand why many of them cannot "come out." Only those professionals who work in the field of parapsychology can be open, as they study psychic and mediumistic experience. Mainstream therapists could lose their credibility if they were open about their psychic experiences. For me this is sad, but it's reality.

Some therapists who do not see themselves as totally mainstream have more spiritually oriented practices. If I were looking for a therapist today, I would look in a New Age magazine or on a New Age website for a professional who has good mainstream medical credentials, but has chosen to be listed in a New Age directory with a business called something like "The Open Heart" or "Spiritual Therapy." Extremely mainstream therapists are not going to list their practices in New Age magazines or on New Age websites. Should you be fortunate enough to have a physician that you know is open to spirit communication, she may have a "spirit-friendly" therapist to recommend.

I would avoid seeing a therapist who believes in spirit but who has no mainstream therapeutic credentials. These days almost anyone can hang up their shingle and say they do counseling. So if you are looking for a therapist, I urge you to check credentials carefully; if you don't, you could end up with a wannabe psychic medium who took a few courses on coaching and now calls herself a counselor.

My Vision of the Perfect Therapist

I like therapists with conventional credentials. The purely metaphysical practitioners are too "only New Age" for me. But that is my personal preference and you may feel differently. For me the perfect therapist would be someone who studied mainstream therapy and has great credentials, but has now ventured outside the boundaries of the traditional therapeutic approach into the New Age world. I call this the *conventional/metaphysical mix.* How is *that* for a new label?

When Interviewing a Therapist

Following is a suggested dialogue to use with a prospective therapist.

"I am looking for a therapist who can help me deal with my emotional issues. One of the things you need to know about me is that I have had psychic experiences and am interested in what many would call the 'paranormal.' While I realize that some of my psychic experiences may be products of my imagination, I also believe that some of these experiences may be authentic. I need a therapist who is comfortable hearing about psychic experiences and who will not automatically assume that I am hallucinating. I also want a therapist who will be frank when she feels that a psychic experience is not authentic. While discussing my psychic experiences is not the main reason I want therapy, I do need to talk about these experiences occasionally.

"I do not expect my therapist to be an expert on psychic experience or even to fully believe in it. But I do need a therapist who is open to psychic experience; otherwise, I would not be comfortable. Do you think you are the right therapist for me?"

Special Challenges for Sensitive People

As a sensitive person, you will pick up on the "vibes" around you, whether they be positive or negative. You may also be exposed to many new ideas as you meet people who are interested in the "spiritual" and "paranormal." As you realize you are coping with more "vibes" and ideas than ever before, you may feel overwhelmed. The good news is that there are people to help you.

Talk to a Professional if You Feel Negative Energies

As I warned earlier, if you have suicidal thoughts, know that this has nothing to do with spirit communication. Seek immediate help from the psychiatric community and go to the ER if necessary. But what about people who experience negative vibes but have no thoughts of harming themselves or others?

If you feel a negative presence around you, get help from a spiritual teacher who believes in spirit communication. The pastor of a Spiritualist church is a good person to talk to. Or make an appointment with an educated, experienced, and respected psychic medium. This is *not* the time to talk to an inexperienced psychic. And this is *not* the time to talk with a close friend who will only become as scared as you are. It is also important to *stay away* from psychics who promise to make that negative energy go away if you pay them hundreds or thousands of dollars. You are better off talking with a Spiritualist minister who will help you evaluate what is happening. In some cases, this minister may feel that your problems are psychological and refer you to a therapist.

I often find that when people report that they are troubled by so-called evil spirits, it is because of energies they are themselves creating, or energies that are being created by people they are associating with. If you feel negative energy around you, you may be creating it by drinking too much or taking drugs that were not prescribed to you.

Another possibility: The negative vibes you are feeling may be connected to your fear of psychic experiences. Many of us were initially scared of the first spirits we saw, but after we got over our fears, we realized the spirits were really a very friendly lot after all!

Like Attracts Like

I have never had a hard time with any so-called negative spirits. I believe in "like attracts like." Spirit communication is sacred. I like to work in Spiritualist churches and in New Age bookstores that are extremely spiritual.

Those of you who in your daily life attract positive friends and work associates are likely to attract positive spirits. Those of you who get into trouble and lead negative lives will most likely feel negative energies around you, and you should not be studying psychic and mediumistic development at this time. An experienced teacher may well suggest that you solve some of your personal issues before joining a development group. *If you are not psychologically stable, this is no time to delve into psychic and mediumistic development. Put that off for a while.* If I were in your shoes, I would pray that all psychic experiences be removed from my being until I was in better psychological condition. Once you have improved your life, your energy will be entirely different, and you will attract only the most positive and glorious spiritual energies. I have seen many change their lives for the better, and if you need to change, I know you *can* if you make up your mind to do so.

Are You an Empath?

An Empath or "empathic person" picks up on the pain and emotions of others, often feeling others' pain in their own bodies and others' emotions in their own minds. While it can be helpful to be intuitive about others, Empaths sometimes experience psychological overload. Psychics and mediums are often Empaths, and while this ability can help us know about the living and about those who have passed on, if we are not able to learn to control the *amount* of empathic feelings we have, we can become exhausted and confused.

In the 1980s, years before I fully realized that I was a medium, my intuitive abilities grew into full-blown empathy and I began to feel the emotional and physical pain of others. I had always sensed what others were going through, but when I started to feel the physical pain of others, I knew this was not healthy. For instance, a friend of mine was going to have surgery on both knees. She went for the surgery on a Monday, and that night, I woke up in the middle of the night with pain in both of my knees. It was real pain, but there was nothing wrong with my knees. I had similar experiences and did not know why. Then in the late '80s and early '90s, when I had visions of spirits and began to understand that I was a medium, I had a sense that somehow these emphatic experiences I was having were related to my opening up as a medium.

When in 1994 I joined a Spiritualist church and sat in development class, my suspicion was confirmed. As I sensed the presence of the spirit of someone who had passed over, I felt the physical symptoms that spirit went through before passing, in *my* body. If a spirit came through who had died of a heart attack, I would feel pain in my chest. I was alarmed and complained to my teacher, who told me that what I was experiencing often happened with beginning students. My teacher reminded me that *I was in charge* and I needed to let the spirits who were communicating through me know that I did *not* need to feel the pain in my body in order to understand an illness. The spirit could let me know the cause of death simply by showing me (within my mind) a picture of the person and lighting up the place on the body where the illness was located. So if a woman had died of lung cancer, I would see an image of the woman and be drawn to her lungs because they were lit up. I didn't have to feel like I was having trouble breathing in order to understand that this woman had lung problems before she passed on.

My teacher helped me understand that I had to *set boundaries with the spirits* and let them know if the sensations they were sending were too strong for me. As I gained control over how much I picked up on, I became more confortable giving readings—and more confident in my ability to take care of myself.

Had I not had the help of a good teacher, I might have decided that my abundance of empathy was a huge emotional problem. It can often be difficult to know whether my thoughts, emotions, and physical symptoms are genuine difficulties that belong to me or if I am being affected by spirit energies. This is an ongoing challenge for mediums, but the more experienced we are, the easier it is for us to separate our feelings from messages from spirit. For psychics, the issues are the same: is the feeling she is having her own or that of her client? The experienced psychic will be better equipped to tell the difference than the beginning student.

Becoming Part of Our "Psychic Community"

When I use the words "our psychic community," I am not talking about any official or organized community. I refer to those of us scattered all over the world who are having psychic and mediumistic experiences. Some of us have close relationships with others in our communities because we have joined spiritual circles that focus on psychic and mediumistic development, or we are part of another spiritual group. I suspect that as you read about people who call themselves mystics, medicine men and women, energy healers, and shamans, you will find that psychics and mediums have similar experiences.

As you open up to your psychic and/or mediumistic gifts, you may start meeting more extra-sensitive people like yourself. Listen carefully to the things your new friends talk about, but do not feel pressure to believe in the same things they believe in. Accept and respect the spiritual journeys they are on, but remember that you are a unique individual and you need to follow your intuition and find your own spiritual path. Your path may or may not turn out to be the path of your closest friend.

I urge you to keep an open mind as you explore psychic and mediumistic experience. Always be ready to learn and willing to change your mind as you glean more information. Beware of the ego within you that may want to be accepted by your friends. That ego can lead you astray and encourage you to take part in activities you do not feel good about. When the need for acceptance and approval becomes stronger than your good common sense, you are in danger of getting caught up in a group you do not belong with. This is how people get trapped in negative groups that begin to rule their lives.

You Do Not Have to Have an Opinion on Everything!

Do you believe in extraterrestrials, Atlantis and Lemuria, the Akashic Record, and alien abductions? These are all subjects that I have feelings about, but I have not studied them in depth enough to feel that I have a right to make statements about whether they are true or not. Many of my colleagues, clients, and readers are upset when I do not give them definitive answers about these things. "You are a medium, so why don't you know?" My answer is "why would I know? And why would I want to make statements about things I have not studied properly?" Because I am an author, conduct readings, and make public appearances, it would be all too easy for me to spout off on subjects I do not know enough about, just to satisfy an audience and make myself look smart. But how irresponsible would that be?

Although I am a psychic and a medium, I do not necessarily believe in all of the ideas that my colleagues embrace. When I say "I do not believe," I add "I do not disbelieve either." I simply do not know. Being able to say "I do not know and you should seek the advice of someone who has thoroughly studied this subject" is a great statement to be able to make. I respect people in the medical field who will admit it when they do not know and then send their patient to a specialist who may have the answer. Being able to say "I do not know" is important for all psychics and mediums.

The Choice Is Yours

If you are blessed to have received psychic and medium-istic gifts, be grateful. Always keep in mind that you have the power to choose whether you want to develop these gifts. If you want to develop them, remember that education is a must. No teacher can make you into a psychic or a medium, but a good teacher will help you learn how to use your talents and teach you about the ethics and responsibilities that go along with your gifts.

No matter whether we choose to develop our gifts or keep them private, remember that we are often more sensitive than others without psychic and mediumistic gifts. We may require more soul searching and help than the average person. If you need help from a spirit-friendly therapist or Spiritualist minister, don't be shy. See help as an opportunity for personal growth.

FIVE

Carole Lynne's Personal Spiritual Toolkit

ALLOW ME TO SHARE with you four important practices that help me the most as I walk my spiritual path. Try them on like clothing in a store and if they do not fit, try a different style until you find what feels comfortable for you. I offer my experience as a starting point; from there you have to take what you want from my suggestions and leave the rest. You need to find your own truth, and if I can help along the way, I am grateful for the opportunity. I am a spiritual seeker on the path, just as you are. We can all learn from each other.

Practice One: Writing in Personal Notebooks

I have had numerous incredible psychic and mediumistic experiences over many years. If I had not taken notes *at the time of the experiences*, years later I would have come to the conclusion that I had made them up or imagined them. Because most of us grew up and live in a society that tries to make us feel as if all psychic and mediumistic experiences are imaginary, it is all too easy for us to discount an experience we once believed was true.

For instance, years ago I had a vision within my mind that a child came to me and told me that he would be born that night. He appeared to me not as a baby, but as the vision of a boy in his early teens. He also told me that I would receive a phone call that night from his father, a good friend of mine, once his mother had gone into labor. I did receive the phone call as predicted, and although I had been sure this baby was going to be a girl, a boy was born. He has grown up to look exactly like he did in my vision that night years ago.

If I had not written about this experience in my notebook, I am sure that within two years I would have decided I had made up the whole thing and that it was a coincidence that the events took place as I saw them in my vision. I continue to take notes to this day.

Practice Two: Live by Spiritualism's Principle of Personal Responsibility

We affirm the moral responsibility of individuals and that they make their own happiness or unhappiness as they obey or disobey Nature's physical and spiritual laws.
—From the American Federation of Spiritualist Churches

I learned this principle from a number of Spiritualist organizations and it has become the cornerstone of my spiritual development. If I had to condense all of my thoughts on how to live a good life into one statement, I would choose this principle.

First let's explore why this principle is so essential in our day-to-day lives, and consider how useful it can be to teach this principle to others, should you choose to work with others as a psychic, medium, or spiritual counselor.

Your Happiness Is Up to You

If we make our own happiness or unhappiness, then there is no one who can save us from our problems or make us happy. You and I are each responsible for our own happiness *or* unhappiness. It goes without saying that good times with others create happy moments in our lives, but ultimately to be happy we need inner happiness that only comes when we take care of ourselves.

Many of us also know that God and spirits can help. However, I have found that when I am helping myself in the most positive ways, God seems to help me the most. It is almost as if I have sent a message out into the universe and the universe responds. I send out positive energy and the universe responds with positive energy. Expressions such as "what goes around comes around" speak to this idea.

Choose Personal Responsibility: Avoid the Blame Game

If we focus on the principle of personal responsibility, we are not able to play *the blame game*. As blame game players, we find reasons to blame everyone and anything we can think of for whatever bothers us. If we have extremely limited financial resources, we blame our families for not being rich. If we do not have any friends, we blame other people for being too hard to get along with. Whatever the challenge, we name and we blame. As we focus on personal responsibility, we will avoid playing this depressing and debilitating game.

Personal Responsibility in Challenging Times

I have found it so interesting to observe the behaviors of people who are experiencing adversity, such as being out of work. Those who are personally responsible immediately start finding positive aspects of unemployment. "Maybe this is the opportunity to find work that I like a lot better than my last job." "This is a time for me to work on my ability to put positive thinking into practice, and get out there and find a job as soon as possible." Responsible people may take a well-deserved vacation before looking for a job, but they do not let too much time elapse before making looking for work their full-time job.

On the other hand, "Blamers" use this adversity as another opportunity to blame the world for their troubles. They blame the person who fired them, the economy, and anything else they can think of. Blamers often use being out of work as a great excuse for doing nothing. "I am on unemployment, and I am going to enjoy it for as long as I can," some say. Many with this mentality become part of the new "garage generation." They stop looking for a job and move into their parents' or friends' garages. They spend endless hours playing computer games when they could make *finding a job their full-time job.* They blame the government, Wall Street, even their parents for creating the dysfunctional family that is destroying their ability to be successful. They blow whatever savings they have on café lattes and upgrading their cell phones.

The harsh words you are reading come from a woman who is very liberal politically. *And of course I know that there are many who need to be on unemployment or disability.* But I cannot close my eyes to what I have seen going on around me by people who take advantage of the help our country offers. Of course there are people out of work who are trying very hard to find a job; I am not talking about them. I am talking about those who are not taking personal responsibility for their lives.

We all know the stories of the boy or girl who grew up in poverty who works hard in school, takes whatever job available, and eventually becomes the head of a multi-million-dollar company. These successes are filled with the energies and vibrations of personal responsibility.

Coping with Health Challenges

For many years I have known an extremely health-challenged woman who takes personal responsibility for her life and her health. She has had brain tumors removed, dealt with cancer twice, and has an autoimmune disease she will cope with for the rest of her life. She does not allow herself to get depressed, but fights for her life each time she has a health challenge. I am awed by her ability to stay positive during the most crucial times. I do not know if I could ever be as positive as she is.

All of us know people with serious health issues who manage their lives successfully. They may not be 100 percent physically healthy, but emotionally and spiritually they are A-plus winners. Many live long lives, despite their genes and their diagnoses!

On the other side of the coin we have the Blamers. When they have health challenges, they blame genetics and tell themselves they do not have a fighting chance. In my opinion, these kinds of beliefs do not help any of us cope with health challenges. Blamers also tend to become depressed and turn to alcohol, drugs, and overeating. Often these addictions lead to poor health and eventually death.

Of course there are those who have tragic lives and even though they have accepted responsibility for their condition, they still die at an early age. We do not understand why such a fate must come to a person who was personally responsible. We also know those who do all the wrong things for their health and live to be ninety-five. *Life is not always just.* However, this occasional lack of justice does *not* give any of us an excuse to stop being as responsible for ourselves—after all, there is a great percentage of people who take care of themselves and do have happier lives.

Ways to Help Others with the Principle of Personal Responsibility

If you ever give readings or work as a spiritual counselor, be prepared for the people who come to you *expecting that you have some kind of mystical power* to change their lives. The truth is that you and I have *no power* to make someone's romantic partner come back; we have no power to make a job materialize. Unfortunately there are psychics out there who charge thousands of dollars and promise to "fix" whatever problem the client has.

The best way you can help clients who ask you to "fix" their problems is to explain *before* you make an appointment that you believe in personal responsibility. Explain that while the guidance from the world of spirit that comes through during a reading can be extremely helpful, *you have no mystical power to solve all their problems.*

If a client seems desperate, suggest psychological help in addition to the reading. In some cases, you may want to suggest that a client put off having a reading until he or she has received medical help. If you do make an appointment with the client, discuss the principle of personal responsibility and encourage the client to do everything possible to better his or her life. If you present this principle with an optimistic attitude, letting the client know that you have confidence in him or her, you may be a tremendous help.

Choice

You and I have a choice. What do we want to create in our lives? Our choices are our responsibility. Over eight years I took written courses from the American Federation of Spiritualist Churches (AFSC), the National Spiritualist Association of Churches (NSAC), and the Spiritualist National Union (SNU). Although the wording of the principle of personal responsibility was slightly different in each organization, the message was the same. This principle is widely practiced by Spiritualists around the world.

Then was then, now is now! Regardless of your past or my past, we are in the present and have to be responsible for ourselves. If we need help, we find the right helpers, work on our problems, and move on!

Practice Three: Regularly Read the Writings of Sri Aurobindo and the Mother

Books by these two great teachers fill the bookcases in my office. I would need to write several more books in order to share what I have learned from them. I will share, in my own words, the most important thing I have learned:

> *While the mind is extremely important and logic and reason are great tools, to achieve spiritual knowledge, happiness, and success, one must go beyond the mind and develop a connection with that Divine spark within that connects each one of us to the Divine.*

The mind *is* a great tool to use as you try to figure out how to drive through the countryside of England or from California to New York. But the mind is not a great tool to use as you aspire to be closer to the Divinity within. Why not? Because the mind throws up too many reasons why this or that may not be so. There you are, having a transcendent moment with glorious spiritual visions, when your mind jumps in and says, "Are you nuts? You're making this up! There is nothing beyond this life on earth. You're deluding yourself!" When you have allowed your inner self to receive spiritual messages in the form of visions, your mind is spoiling the whole experience. The mind is *sure* that it knows everything, and if the mind cannot understand something, then it must not exist. (Sounds a bit like science, doesn't it?)

Following is a quote by Sri Aurobindo that helped me accept that my mind is not the highest authority. I have bolded some of the words in his quotes. Some words in the quotes may not be familiar to you if you have not studied Sri Aurobindo and the Mother extensively. However, the quotes are still extremely helpful.

Sri Aurobindo writes:

> *I would ask one simple question of those who would make the intellectual mind the standard and judge of spiritual experience.* **Is the Divine something less than mind or is it something greater?** *Is mental consciousness with its groping enquiry, endless argument, unquenchable doubt, stiff and unplastic logic something superior or even equal to the Divine Consciousness or is it something inferior in its action and status? If it is greater, then there is no reason to seek after the Divine. If it is equal, then spiritual experience is quite superfluous. But if it is inferior, how can it challenge, judge, make the Divine stand as an accused or a witness before its tribunal, summon it to appear as a candidate for admission before a Board of Examiners or pin it like an insect under its examining microscope? Can the vital animal hold up as infallible the standard*

of its vital instincts, associations and impulses, and judge, interpret and fathom by it the mind of man? It cannot, because man's mind is a greater power working in a wider, more complex way which the animal vital consciousness cannot follow. **Is it so difficult to see, similarly, that the Divine Consciousness must be something infinitely wider, more complex than the human mind, filled with greater powers and lights, moving in a way which mere mind cannot judge, interpret or fathom by the standard of its fallible reason and limited half-knowledge?** The simple fact is there that Spirit and Mind are not the same thing and that it is the spiritual consciousness into which the yogin has to enter (in all this I am not in the least speaking of the supermind), if he wants to be in permanent contact or union with the Divine. It is not then a freak of the Divine or a tyranny **to insist on the mind recognizing its limitations,** quieting itself, giving up its demands, and opening and surrendering to a greater Light than it can find on its own obscurer level.

This doesn't mean that mind has no place at all in the spiritual life; but it means that it cannot be even the main instrument, much less the authority, to whose judgment all must submit itself, including the Divine. Mind must learn from the greater consciousness it is approaching and not impose its own standards on it; it has to receive illumination, open to a higher Truth, admit *a greater power that doesn't work according to mental canons, surrender itself and allow its half-light half-darkness to be flooded from above till where it was blind it can see, where it was deaf it can hear, where it was insensible it can feel, and where it was baffled, uncertain, questioning, disappointed it can have joy, fulfillment, certitude and peace.*

This is the position on which yoga stands, a position based upon constant experience since men began to seek after the Divine.

—Sri Aurobindo [SABCL, 22:170-171]

Many readers of Sri Aurobindo would agree that he is not the easiest writer to read. But take the time to read this quote over and over. Not only will you better understand his words, but you may also feel the spiritual power that emanates from them. I cannot begin to tell you how much this teacher's books have helped me on the spiritual path!

Aurobindo has also helped me to accept that walking the spiritual path is a lifetime process. If I grasp at spiritual experiences and ideas and label them "the absolute truth," I will have stopped along the way and may not continue into the Unknowable.

Here is a quote from "The Life Divine" by Sri Aurobindo:

An Unknowable which appears to us in many states and attributes of being, in many forms of consciousness, in many activities of energy, this is what the Mind can ultimately say about the existence which

we ourselves are and which we see in all that is
presented to our thoughts and senses. It is in and
through those states, those forms, those activities that
we have to approach and know the Unknowable.
But if in our haste to arrive at a Unity that
our mind can seize and hold, if in our insis-
tence to confine the Infinite in our embrace
we identify the Reality with any one definable
state of being however pure and eternal, with
any particular attribute however general and
comprehensive with any fixed formulation of
consciousness however vast in its scope, with
any energy or activity however boundless its
application, and if we exclude all the rest, *then*
our thoughts sin against Its unknowableness and
arrive not at a true unity but at a division of the
Indivisible.

Read this quote again and again. Its incredible power
and meaning may become part of you. You may also find it
helpful to read the quotes out loud.

Following are several of my favorite quotes from the
Mother, who, along with Sri Aurobindo, founded the Sri
Aurobindo Ashram and the Sri Aurobindo Society.

The Mother has helped me to cultivate patience. Many
of her quotes, in her books and on the Sri Aurobindo Society website, are transcriptions from talks that she gave to
her students at the Sri Aurobindo Ashram. Here is one of
my favorites:

When one aspires for something, if at the same time one knows that the aspiration will be heard and answered in the best way possible, that establishes a quietude in the being, a quietude in its vibrations; whilst if there is a doubt, an uncertainty, if one does not know what will lead one to the goal or if ever one will reach it or whether there is a way of doing so, and so on, then one gets disturbed and that usually creates a sort of little whirlwind around the being, which prevents it from receiving the real thing. Instead, if one has a quiet faith, if whilst aspiring one knows that there is no aspiration (naturally, sincere aspiration) which remains unanswered, then one is quiet. One aspires with as much fervor as possible, but does not stand in nervous agitation asking oneself why one does not get immediately what one has asked for. One knows how to wait. I have said somewhere: "To know how to wait is to put time on one's side." That is quite true. For if one gets excited, one loses all one's time—one loses one's time, loses one's energy, loses one's movements. To be very quiet, calm, peaceful, with the faith that what is true will take place, and that if one lets it happen, it will happen so much the quicker. Then, in that peace everything goes much better.

—The Mother [CWMCE, 5:396-97]

I read this quote whenever the problems of my everyday life begin to put me in a frazzled state. As an extremely sensitive person, I can be in a state of peace and calm in one moment, and agitated in the next—when, say, a remark or an email comes to me that upsets me so terribly that you would not know it was still "me." I react physically and emotionally, and while I understand that I am allowing the remark or email to upset me, I do not have consistent control over my reactions.

I am still working on becoming a balanced person, and although by this time I am doing very well, I still have a ways to go! Becoming balanced is a lifetime process. Quotes by the Mother always help to put me back on the track of peace and avoid negative influences. This quote by the Mother about *sincerity* helps me get in touch with the Divine spark within.

A student asked the Mother: "What is the fundamental virtue to be cultivated in order to prepare for the spiritual life?"

> *I have said this many times, but this is an opportunity to repeat it: it is sincerity. A sincerity which must become total and absolute, for sincerity alone is your protection on the spiritual path. If you are not sincere, at the very next step you are sure to fall and break your head. All kinds of forces, wills, influences, entities are there, on the look-out for the least little rift in this sincerity and they immediately rush in through that rift and begin to throw you into confusion. Therefore, before doing anything, beginning anything, trying anything, be sure first of all that you are not only as sincere as you can be, but have the intention of becoming still more so.*

For that is your only protection.
—The Mother [CWMCE, 8:248-49]

While I do not have experience with what some would call "evil spirits," I have felt the influences of negativity around me at times, especially in public places or in the company of people who do not live positive lives. I firmly believe that when I feel these unhealthy influences, I can protect myself from them by focusing on the Divine Consciousness and getting in touch with the spark of Divinity within each one of us. I believe that this is the kind of protection the Mother speaks of.

I do not perform the complicated rituals used by many psychics and mediums for protection before they do readings. In fact, I sense that doing complicated protection rituals only creates fear within me and announces to the world of spirit that I am so fearful that I *must* do a ritual. I feel more comfortable saying a prayer of gratitude and asking that the Divine help me to do the best work possible for my client. Many psychics, mediums, and healers who do rituals of protection would disagree with me; I want to emphasize that what I have just shared is my personal experience.

When I am approaching a difficult situation in my life, getting in touch with the essence of Divinity is my biggest protection. I prefer simple and sincere prayer over rituals for protection. Following is a quote that helps me when I am upset and need to get distance from a situation.

Most of you live on the surface of your being, exposed to the touch of external influences. You live almost projected, as it were, outside your own body, and when you meet some unpleasant being similarly projected you get upset. The whole trouble arises out of your not being accustomed to stepping back. You must always step back into yourself—learn to go deep within—step back and you will be safe. Do not lend yourself to the superficial forces which move in the outside world. Even if you are in a hurry to do something, step back for a while and you will discover to your surprise how much sooner and with what greater success your work can be done. If someone is angry with you, do not be caught in his vibrations but simply step back and his anger, finding no support or response, will vanish. Always keep your peace, resist all temptation to lose it. **Never decide anything without stepping back, never speak a word without stepping back, never throw yourself into action without stepping back. All that belongs to the ordinary world is impermanent and fugitive, so there is nothing in it worth getting upset about. What is lasting, eternal, immortal and infinite—that indeed is worth having, worth conquering, worth possessing.** It is Divine Light, Divine Love, Divine Life—it is also Supreme Peace, Perfect Joy and All-Mastery upon earth with the Complete Manifestation as the crowning. When you get the sense of the relativity of things, then whatever happens you can step back and look; you can remain quiet and call on the Divine Force and wait for an answer. Then you

will know exactly what to do. Remember, therefore,
that you cannot receive the answer before you are
very peaceful. ***Practice that inner peace, make***
at least a small beginning and go on in your
practice until it becomes a habit with you.
—The Mother [CWMCE, 3:160]

The word "habit" in the last sentence of this quote
jumps out at me. We are mistaken when we think that if
we do something once, we have learned it. It is repetition
that creates a habit! When we are faced with a difficult situation, our emotions can control us; it may be difficult to
"step back" and have a calmer view. *We have to step back*
over and over until it becomes a habit!

I'll close with one more beautiful quote from the Mother.

So long as outward circumstances will have the
power to upset you, you will not be able to keep
the Lord's peace and joy. To have them perma-
nently, you must live in your inner consciousness,
deep inside and care only for your aspiration and
the Lord's presence.
—The Mother [p-170, White Roses, Sixth
Edition, 1999]

In the References section of this book, you will find
contact information for the Sri Aurobindo Society. Be sure
to check out the SABDA bookstore on their website.

Practice Four: Refer to My "Top Priority" List

I read the following list again and again in order to stay focused on the essentials of living a good life. Needless to say, I have accomplished more with some things on this list than others, but I continue to work on every item on this list, even though I realize accomplishing these tasks is a lifetime project.

1. Take care of your body with proper nutrition, exercise, and sleep. If you do not have enough energy, it will be hard to be positive.

2. Put your "stuff" in order. Clean out your house, and if you have a car, clean it up. Throw out the things you do not need or find a safe storage space. A cluttered home and car create a cluttered mind.

3. Consider making the hard changes. If you need a new job or new place to live, start working towards this change. If you are in an unhappy relationship, get the help you need to make the relationship work better, or consider getting out of the relationship. Always get the help you need from family, friends, or professionals when it is time to make the hard choices and changes.

4. Change your mind. When you have negative thoughts, give yourself a time limit and then think about something else—something more positive.

5. Discover what triggers your negative thoughts and feelings. Who makes you angry, who irritates you, who makes you feel jealous? Actually,

no one *makes* you create negative thoughts and feelings—you do. But if certain people and situations are identified as triggers of negativity for you, either learn to react in a more positive way or limit your time with those people and situations until you can respond more positively.

My list helps me refocus on the positive. Perhaps you would like to make a list of your own. Feel free to use any of the items on my list, and add additional items. Always remember to go easy on yourself. Self-improvement is a lifelong process.

Conclusion

Following is a poem I wrote for all of us who are on the spiritual path and trying to improve our lives.

You are the magic
You are the answer
The spark of Divinity lives in your heart
You make it happen
You are creation
It is all up to you, It is all up to you.

Destiny rides at your side in the play
On the lower rung of fate
Find the seed of Divinity in your soul
Riding your highest realms

Outride Destiny
Create Reality

Fate is the default for those with no power
Ride with the Divine
Your soul will reach out
Fly high to the wisdom, the realms of infinity
On wings of wonder
Find Peace, Find Peace

Conclusion

My Dear Friends,

I was inspired to write this book by those of you who have asked me "am I psychic or am I making it up?" I've heard this question over and over again. It is my sincere hope that reading this book has helped you to answer that question and many others. I also know that as a question has been answered, another question takes its place. *Questions are the staples of spiritual life!*

Over the years, I have come to know many of you who email, phone, and chat with me online better than I know many of my neighbors. Some of you have become clients and students. We share a huge common interest: our spiritual experiences.

In today's world of the Internet, the conclusion of this book does not have to be the end of our connection: **ultimately** a blog conversation between us will reach beyond the **parameters** of this book. Please visit my blog at *www.communicatingwithspirit.wordpress.com* and my new site at *www.worldpsychicsoul.com*.

For now, here are some special thoughts from me to you as we come to the conclusion of this book.

Embrace the Light Within

Each of us is a spirit living within a physical body. When we are ready to let go of the physical, the spirit within makes a transition into eternal life. It is the spirit within that makes it possible for us to experience our psychic and mediumistic nature. Each one of us is part of the Divine Consciousness whom many call God, which has created and continues to manifest All That Is. You have within you the light of all potentials. You must embrace this light in order to know who you are and what you are called to do in this lifetime. Do you allow the Divine (the God of your understanding) to speak to you? Are you open to messages from the Divine?

Practice Faith and Patience

I have received messages from the Divine that have been hard for me to cope with, as I have not always had instant proof of why a message was important. For instance, about seven years ago as I left Puerto Rico after spending a week doing readings and demonstrations of mediumship, I felt the Divine telling me to learn to speak Spanish. And so I got an audiotape course and began. I did not progress quickly and after a while gave up, deciding it was not really so important after all.

But these messages from the Divine kept coming back to me and telling me to learn Spanish. I was resistant because I was so busy doing other things and could see no reason to learn the language. Then the phone started ringing with prospective clients on the other end of the line asking me "Do you speak Spanish?" This happened more times than I could chalk up to coincidence, and one day I banged my hand on a table and said to myself, "OK, that is *it*! I am meant to learn Spanish—these messages will not go away, and now people are being impressed to call me and ask if I speak Spanish."

Since that time I have purchased another Spanish course, and slowly but surely, I am learning Spanish. As a matter of fact, I recently stayed in a US hotel, and quite a few bilingual Spanish and English speakers were working there. I was able to hold conversations with them in Spanish. They took me under their wings and became instant Spanish teachers, correcting me when they knew I could say something in a better way. It was very exciting!

Not Knowing Why Is Hard for Me

In the scenario discussed in the last section, I did not know why I was meant to learn Spanish, and this off-and-on romance continued over many years without my making a full commitment to learning it. It was time for me to surrender and trust that learning Spanish was a calling, just as I had to trust that becoming a professional medium was a calling. When I first started working as a medium, I was afraid because I did not know how my life would change or if I would be able to connect with spirit again and again. I had to trust the Divine. Before I started learning Spanish, I had to trust the Divine and accept that I would not really know why or where this would take me. As I continue to go through the process of learning the language, I wonder whether I will ultimately be a bilingual medium, doing sessions in Spanish (perhaps with a translator to help me with things that are too hard for me to express in Spanish). My journey with Spanish is a mystical adventure for me that requires *faith and trust in the Divine*. I share this story with you because there may be things in your own spiritual experience that you do not yet understand. *Not knowing why* may also be difficult for you.

Not Knowing Is a Special Realm

In some ways, "not knowing why" puts us outside the box of our regular thoughts. Some people call this "thinking outside the box," and this experience often generates extremely creative ideas in people. What I am talking about now is different. I am not talking about *thinking* outside the box, but simply *being* outside the box—*existing* outside the box. When I am outside the box, time seems to stop, thoughts become softer, and I can float up into a higher state of consciousness fairly easily.

The state of "not knowing why" puts me outside the circle of control I like to feel I have over my life. However, once outside this circle, I find myself in a spiritual environment where it is easier to hear the voice of the Divine and get in touch with the Divine spark within.

If you are reading these words and looking for some kind of proof and logic, you will not find it. These words are inspirational. And it is inspiration, not logic, that will take me (and in my opinion, also take you) into a state of higher consciousness. Inspiration can help us to let go of always needing an answer to every question we have about the universe. Inspiration helps us to accept a certain amount of "not knowing" in our lives. Of course we are not throwing out logic and reason entirely, as they are the basic tools that we need to get along in life. But we also need inspiration so that we can let down the barriers that separate us from our true inner spirits. *It is ironic that as we allow ourselves to not know why, knowing comes to us.*

The Most Important Spiritual Site Is YOU

As you explore your spiritual side, remember that what you are looking for is within. If you can travel to spiritual sites around the world, that is a real luxury, but travel is not necessary. The most important site is *you*. I have found that even after traveling to some of the most spiritual sites in the world, I have the clearest and deepest connection to the Divine when I am in my humble home office, meditating, singing, giving readings, or teaching spiritual classes! My clients and students on the spiritual path are my best companions and the energy we create together is perfect.

You are part of the Divine Creative Force and all that you need is within you. However, you will only realize your potential with deep introspection. Get to know yourself really well. As you become familiar with your individual nature, you will discover your talents. As you discover your talents, you can organize yourself to find out how to learn the skills that you need in order to share your talents with the world.

Are You Psychic or Making It Up?

If you have reached the conclusion of this book, I'll bet you have had some authentic psychic and mediumistic experiences. From time to time, all of us add things to these experiences from our own minds. Remember that understanding, developing, and refining your spiritual gifts is a lifelong process. Even the most professional psychics and mediums have to work at separating their own thoughts, the thoughts of others, and authentic messages from spirit. This task comes with the territory.

My thoughts are with you as you learn more about your spiritual gifts. My prayers are also with you as you educate your friends and loved ones in order to enlist their support. Always remember that everyone you know does not have to believe you in order for your experiences to be real.

Perhaps you have loved ones who will benefit from reading all or parts of this book. Be kind to your skeptical friends. Help them to understand you, rather than pushing them away because they do not "see" as you do.

Remember that if you have been given the gift of being able to see the world of spirit, this is a blessing. Yes, you do have to take special care of your extra-sensitive self. It is important to be around positive environments and positive people. Make the necessary lifestyle changes in order to be healthy physically, emotionally, and spiritually and you will find joy and happiness. You will also bring joy to others.

Above all, enjoy your life. While I am so grateful to be able to connect with the world of spirit to bring through messages from those who have passed on and guidance from the higher realms, I also love to spend time playing my guitar, going out to karaoke clubs to sing, and cooking the food I love. I enjoy my family and friends—some who "see" as I do, but most who do not. Know that it is important to find balance in your life. As you open up to the world of spirit, you will find it a beautiful place to connect with, but so is the earth you walk on each day. Do not become overly involved with the world of spirit or you will miss too much of the earth life you are living. Find balance and more balance and you will be a happy psychic.

May peace be with you always and eternally,

Carole Lynne

Organization Resources

Following is a list of organizations that have wonderful bookstores. Visit their websites to see their reading lists. Many of these organizations also have correspondence courses or seminars that you can attend at their locations.

The National Spiritualist Association of Churches (NSAC)

The NSAC website provides a state-by-state directory of their many Spiritualist churches. You can also learn about their correspondence courses through the Morris Pratt Institute. Both members and non-members can take courses.

National Spiritualist Association of Churches
13 Cottage Row
PO Box 217
Lily Dale, NY 14752
USA
Phone: 716-595-2000
Website: *http://www.nsac.org*
NSAC has a fantastic online bookstore.

The American Federation of Spiritualist Churches

This small federation has several churches in the United States. The correspondence courses are some of the best I have taken on Spiritualism. Both members and non-members can take courses. Reverend Doctor Irene Harding, co-pastor at the Plymouth Spiritualist Church in Plymouth, MA, is head of the education department. Visit the AFSC website and the Plymouth Spiritualist Church website to learn more about the locations of their churches and their courses.

AFSC
Website: *http://www.afschurches.com/*

Plymouth Spiritualist Church
Rev. Dr. Irene I. Harding
AFSC Dean of Education
PO Box 1840
Sagamore Beach, MA 02562
Phone: 508-888-6049
Email: *iharding18@comcast.net*

The Spiritualist National Union of Great Britain

This organization offers courses at the Arthur Findlay College in Stansted, England. It is a beautiful place to study and the grounds are magnificent. Students from all over the world attend weeklong courses. Members and non-members can take correspondence courses. Their bookstore has many books on Spiritualism and other spiritual topics. Write or call the college and request a booklist.

Arthur Findlay College
Stansted Hall
Stansted Mountfitchet
Essex
United Kingdom
CM24 8UD
Phone: 01279-813636
Website: *http://www.arthurfindlaycollege.org*

The Sri Aurobindo Society

SAS has a beautiful Ashram in Pondicherry, India. Guests from around the world come to Pondicherry and stay in one of the SAS guesthouses. The SAS website is an inspiration to all who regularly visit, and you can sign up for their monthly newsletters.

The best place to buy books by Sri Aurobindo and the Mother in India is at SABDA. The Sri Aurobindo Ashram publication department publishes the works of Sri Aurobindo and the Mother as well as books by disciples on their life and teachings, in over fifteen languages. The publications department's distribution unit is SABDA. Apart from the Sri Aurobindo Ashram publications, SABDA also distributes books of other publishers with related content. SABDA has two retail outlets: Service branch inside the Sri Aurobindo Ashram main building, and Kripa branch diagonally opposite from it.

17 Rue de la Marine (next to the Kripa branch)
Sri Aurobindo Ashram
Pondicherry 605002
India
Phone: +91 413 2223328, 22333656
Fax: +91 413 2223328
Website: *http://www.sabda.in*

Lotus Press is the best place to buy books by Sri Aurobindo and the Mother in the United States, with a huge selection of works by both authors.

Lotus Press
PO Box 325
Twin Lakes, WI 53181
Phone: 800-824-6396
Phone: 262-889-8561
Website: *http://www.lotuspress.com*

About the Author

Carole Lynne was quite happy working as a performing artist and running a company called Quality Performance Coaching. She traveled around the United States as a musician and coached businesspeople and educators in giving presentations and lectures. Little did she know that in midlife, spirits would begin appearing to her.

Carole Lynne wanted to understand more about her spiritual gifts. She took many Spiritualist courses from the National Spiritualist Association of Churches, the American Federation of Spiritualist Churches, and the Spiritualist National Union of Great Britain. She is certified in the United States as an ordained minister, commissioned healer, and certified medium; she is also a CSNU award-holder in public speaking and mediumship demonstration with the SNU of Great Britain.

Carole Lynne believes that there is much to be learned by studying many spiritual pathways. At present, she studies and is influenced by the works of Sri Aurobindo and the Mother, founders of the Sri Aurobindo Society and Ashram in Pondicherry, India. She is also studying the books of Kyriacos Markides, a professor at the University of Maine who has written books on Christian mysticism. Markides has spent many years traveling to Mount Athos to interview and write about the monks. Carole Lynne is happy that her religion of Spiritualism encourages its members to be open to the Truth to be found in many religions.

In addition to *Are You Psychic or Making It Up?*, Carole Lynne is the author of *How to Get a Good Reading from a Psychic Medium, Heart and Sound, Consult Your Inner Psychic,* and *Cosmic Connection: Messages for a Better World.*

Carole Lynne is featured on the prestigious website *BestPsychicMediums.com* and has been on ABC News, Fox News, and numerous Internet radio programs. Ms. Lynne is an award-holder with the Coalition of Visionary Resources for her book *Consult Your Inner Psychic.*

Carole Lynne lives in Massachusetts and Maui.

Visit the following websites for information on Carole Lynne, her work, and her books:

www.carolelynne.com (main website)
www.worldpsychicsoul.com (sister website)
www.bestpsychicmediums.com (featured on this site)
www.communicatingwithspirit.wordpress.com (a blog)
Email: *carolelynne777@carolelynne.com*
Phone: 617-964-0058

How Carole Lynne's Books Can Help You

Whenever I appear at an event to do a demonstration of spirit communication or conduct a seminar for aspiring students, I give them a brief description of each of my books and how each particular book can be useful. People have found these descriptions helpful and hopefully you will also.

Heart and Sound

A book of affirmations, prayers, and chants with an accompanying CD of the chants.

This product is beautifully packaged and makes an incredible gift for you or a friend. The affirmations and prayers are very healing and helpful to those who are going through changes in their lives, or experiencing grief. The chants on the CD are all original channeled chants in English that you can listen to or sing along with. Many teachers and spiritual circle leaders use the CD with their groups. Everyone in the circle can "sing along" with me. Some of the chants are soft and healing while others are energizing.

How to Get a Good Reading from a Psychic Medium

Need to know more about the different kinds of readings offered by psychics and mediums? Read this book before making an appointment with one.

Some people have called this "the consumer's guide to getting readings." The book is full of information you need to know before making an appointment for a psychic or mediumistic reading. Unfortunately, there are far too many untalented readers out there who are ready to take your money. This book will help you as you choose an educated, experienced, and ethical reader.

Consult Your Inner Psychic

If you want to get more in touch with your inner spirit, this book and enclosed CD will be of great help to you.

CYIP is a divination product. You learn about the twelve Energies and four States of Being. Then you can give yourself an intuitive reading: you ask a question and choose one of the twelve Energies and one of the four States of Being. The combination of the chosen Energy and State of Being leads you to your Message, which is the answer to the question you asked. The instructions in the book are easy to follow! As you get better and better at tuning in to your own intuition, you will see how the readings you give yourself are more exact answers to the question you asked. Using the product is not like giving yourself a tarot card reading—it's more like an I Ching reading. I used this product almost every day for a year, and the experience changed my life for the better.

Online *Consult Your Inner Psychic* Product: visit *www.carolelynne.com* and read about the "Online Reading." This product is based on the *Consult Your Inner Psychic* book. Order this product and give yourself a reading online everyday of the week if you like. It is very good exercise for your intuition and lots of fun. My website offers a special discount.

Cosmic Connection: Messages for a Better World

If you are opening up to the world of spirit, this may be the perfect time to read my story. In this book I share all of my most important spiritual experiences. Clients and students who have read this book let me know that they had many "ah-ha" moments of recognition as they read the book. I receive reports that reading my story helped many readers accept their own experiences.

If spirit speaks to you in a creative manner through poetry, music, or art, you will find this book very appealing. Many of my spiritual experiences have been through creativity.

To Our Readers

Weiser Books, an imprint of Red Wheel/Weiser, publishes books across the entire spectrum of occult, esoteric, speculative, and New Age subjects. Our mission is to publish quality books that will make a difference in people's lives without advocating any one particular path or field of study. We value the integrity, originality, and depth of knowledge of our authors.

Our readers are our most important resource, and we appreciate your input, suggestions, and ideas about what you would like to see published.

Visit our website at *www.redwheelweiser.com* to learn about our upcoming books and free downloads, and be sure to go to *www.redwheelweiser.com/newsletter* to sign up for newsletters and exclusive offers.

You can also contact us at *info@rwwbooks.com* or at

Red Wheel/Weiser, LLC
665 Third Street, Suite 400
San Francisco, CA 94107